Developing Skills for the TOEFL® iBT
Second Edition

Intermediate **READING**

Developing Skills for the TOEFL® iBT Second Edition

`READING`

Paul Edmunds · Nancie McKinnon · Jeff Zeter

© 2009 Compass Publishing

Acquisitions Editor: Tanya Shawlinski
Content Editor: J.K. Runner
Development Editors: David Charlton
Cover/Interior Design: Design Plus

Email: info@compasspub.com
http://www.compasspub.com

ISBN: 978-1-59966-352-4

27 26 25 24 23 22 21 20 19 18
18 17 16 15 14

Printed in Korea

Second Edition

Developing Skills for the TOEFL® iBT

Intermediate

READING

Compass Publishing

Paul Edmunds · Nancie McKinnon · Jeff Zeter

Table of Contents

Introduction to the TOEFL® iBT ——————————— 6

The TOEFL® iBT Reading Section ——————— 11

Preview Test ————————————————————— 15

Chapter 1 Fact Questions ————————————— 21

Chapter 2 Negative Fact Questions ——————— 35

Chapter 3 Inference Questions ————————— 49

Chapter 4 Rhetorical Purpose Questions ———— 63

Vocabulary Review 1 ————————————————— 76

Mini Test 1 ————————————————————————— 78

Chapter 5 Vocabulary Questions ——————— 83

Chapter 6 Reference Questions ———————— 97

Chapter 7 Sentence Simplification Questions —— 111

Chapter 8 Text Insertion Questions —————— 125

Vocabulary Review 2 ———————————————— 138

Mini Test 2 ——————————————————————— 140

Chapter 9 Prose Summary Questions —————— 145

Chapter 10 Table/Chart Questions ——————— 159

Vocabulary Review 3 ———————————————— 172

Mini Test 3 ——————————————————————— 174

Practice Test ——————————————————— 183

Answer Key

Introduction to the TOEFL® iBT

What to Expect on the TOEFL®

The TOEFL® (Test of English as a Foreign Language) is an Internet-based test designed to assess English proficiency in non-native speakers who want to achieve academic success and communicate effectively in English. Most people take the TOEFL® iBT to gain admission into universities and colleges where instruction is in English. Additionally, many employers and government agencies use the scores to determine a person's English ability. It is not meant to test academic knowledge or computer ability, and as such, questions are always based on information found in the test (computer tutorials are available for those not familiar with personal computers). We have designed this practice book to be as similar as possible to the actual TOEFL® iBT in format and appearance in order to better prepare you for the test.

The TOEFL® iBT is divided into four sections: reading, listening, speaking, and writing.

Major Changes to the Internet-Based TOEFL® (iBT)

- **General**
  - ⇨ The test measures all four language skills equally; a speaking section is included.
  - ⇨ The Test of Spoken English® (TSE®) will now be part of the TOEFL®. Test takers will no longer take the TSE® as a separate test.
  - ⇨ Order of sections on the test:

    Reading

    Listening

    (10-minute break)

    Speaking

    Writing
  - ⇨ The test is approximately four hours long and is taken in one day.
  - ⇨ Tests are administered through the Internet in Educational Testing Service (ETS) test centers around the world.
  - ⇨ There is no structure section, as there was in previous tests.
  - ⇨ Note-taking is allowed in every section, and is not marked.
  - ⇨ The test is a linear exam, not computer adaptive; each test taker receives the same range of questions.
  - ⇨ The scores will be viewed online.

- **Reading / Listening**
  - ⇨ Passages for the reading and listening sections are longer than those in the computer-based test (CBT). Refer to the introduction of individual sections for further details.

Speaking / Writing

⇨ Tasks for the speaking and writing sections include integrated questions that require more than one skill to complete, i.e., reading and/or listening, then speaking or writing.

⇨ For the speaking section, test takers speak into a microphone, and their responses are digitized and sent to the ETS Online Scoring Network.

⇨ For the writing section, test takers must type their responses.

The TOEFL® iBT Format

Section	Number of Questions	Time (minutes)	Score
Reading	3–5 passages • 12–14 questions each • 700 words per passage	60–100	30 points
Listening	4–6 lectures • 6 questions each • 500–800 words (4–6 min.) 2–3 conversations • 5 questions each • 400–500 words (2–3 min.)	60–90	30 points
BREAK		10	
Speaking	2 independent tasks • 1 personal experience • 1 preference/choice 2 integrated tasks (Read Listen Speak) • Reading 100 words • Conversation 200 words (1–2 min.) • Lecture 200–300 words (1–2 min.) 2 integrated tasks (Listen-Speak) • Conversation 200 words (1–2 min.) • Lecture 200–300 words (1–2 min.)	20	30 points
Writing	1 independent task 1 integrated task (Read-Listen-Write) - Reading 250–300 words - Lecture 250–300 words (2 min.)	50	30 points

Study Tips

The only way to be certain of an excellent TOEFL® score is to be able to read, write, understand, and speak English like an educated native speaker. You have no doubt been developing your ability in these areas for many years now. Unfortunately, this is not something one can accomplish by studying in the traditional way. However, research conducted over the years by applied linguists, psychologists, and educators has yielded a considerable amount of information on the best methods for refining these skills for the purposes of standardized tests. By keeping the following study tips in mind, you can optimize your study habits and achieve the highest possible scores with the level of language proficiency you have obtained.

- Prepare a study area for yourself. This should include the following:
  - ⇨ A comfortable chair and spacious table or desk
  - ⇨ Suitable lighting
  - ⇨ Good ventilation and air quality — an open window or a house plant are good ideas
  - ⇨ An area free of distractions such as outside noise, television, or radio (unless you are using the television or radio to study)
  - ⇨ Proper space to keep all the materials you will need when studying, such as books, paper, pens, pencils, a tape recorder or other recording device, and if possible, a computer with Internet access

- Study regularly over a long period of time. Do not study to the point of exhaustion, as this has been shown to be ineffective in retaining information.

- "Cramming," i.e., studying intensely for a day or two before an exam, is not effective, as it strains your general health and well-being and does not lead to good long-term retention of information or skills.

- Psychologists have discovered a principle called "state-specific memory." This means you remember things better in the same conditions that you learned them. For example, if you always study math at night, you will do better on a math exam taken at night. Use this concept to your advantage. If you know when and under what conditions you will take the TOEFL®, simulate these in your study environment and habits. For instance, if you plan to take the TOEFL® on a Saturday afternoon, then make a point to study in the afternoons.

- Be well rested on the day of the exam. Do not stay up all night studying. Also, eat healthy foods including fruits and vegetables.

- Be relaxed and confident. Do the best that you can and do not worry excessively about any mistakes or uncertainties.

Registering For the TOEFL®

Students must get registration information for the TOEFL®. Registration information can be obtained online at the ETS website. The Internet address is www.ets.org/toefl. The website provides information such as testing locations, costs, and identification requirements. The website also provides other test-preparation material.

The registration information, such as the test center location, identification requirements, and costs, will vary depending on the country in which you take the test. Be sure to follow these requirements carefully. If you do not have the proper requirements in order, you may not be able to take the test. Remember that if you register online, you will need to have your credit card information ready.

What TOEFL® Scores Are Used For

The primary use of TOEFL® scores is for acceptance into universities, colleges, and other institutions where English is the main language of instruction. It is estimated that about 4,400 such institutions require TOEFL® scores for admission.

The highest possible score on the iBT is 120 points. Different institutions will have their own specific score requirements for admission. For that reason, it is very important to check with each institution individually to find out what its admission requirements are. For example, a passing score at one university may not be a passing score at another university. It is the responsibility of the student to find out what the requirements are for each institution.

Although TOEFL® scores are used primarily to satisfy the admissions requirements of universities, they are also necessary when applying for certain kinds of jobs. Many government agencies as well as multinational corporations require applicants to submit TOEFL® scores. Even English-teaching institutes may request TOEFL® scores in order to place students at the appropriate level of instruction.

Certainly, doing well on the TOEFL® can be very helpful for students in both their academic and professional careers. However, success requires consistent and dedicated practice. We hope that you will take full advantage of this practice book and study hard. Your hard work and dedication will provide you with the best opportunity to do well on the TOEFL® and meet your goals for the future.

Academic Subjects in the TOEFL®

The following is a list of academic subject areas typically seen in the TOEFL®:

Humanities	Social Sciences	Biological Sciences	Physical Sciences
Archaeology	Anthropology	Agriculture	Astronomy
Architecture	Business	Anatomy	Chemistry
Art History	Economics	Biology	Computer Science
Fine Arts	Education	Botany	Engineering
Linguistics	Geography	Entomology	Geology
Literature	History	Environmental Science	Mathematics
Music	Political Science	Medicine	Oceanography
Philosophy	Psychology	Zoology	Physics
	Public Health		
	Sociology		
	Urban Studies		

The TOEFL® iBT Reading Section

In the reading section of the TOEFL® iBT, you will be required to read three to five passages on varying topics. After each passage, you will answer twelve to fourteen questions that test your ability to understand vocabulary, sentence structure, and factual information, as well as implied information and the writer's intention. You will not see the questions until after you have read the passage. While answering the questions, you will be permitted to look back at the reading. You do not need any previous knowledge on the topic in order to answer the questions correctly.

- **Passage Types**
  1. Exposition – Material that provides information about or an explanation of a topic
  2. Argumentation – Material that presents a point of view about a topic and provides supporting evidence in favor of a position
  3. Narrative – An account of a person's life or a historical event

- **Question Types**
  Questions in the reading section of the TOEFL® iBT are multiple choice and much like those found in older versions of the TOEFL®. The following list explains the question types and number of each type on the test. Questions will not necessarily appear in this order.

Question Type	Number	Task
Factual Information	3-6	Select details or facts provided in the passage.
Negative Factual Information	0-2	Identify something that is not in the passage or not true according to the passage.
Inference	0-2	Select an answer based on information not actually stated in the passage, but that is implied or can be inferred.
Rhetorical Purpose	0-2	Identify the author's method in explaining a point, or why the author has mentioned something.
Vocabulary	3-5	Choose the best synonym.
Pronoun Reference	0-2	Identify the noun to which a pronoun refers.
Sentence Simplification	0-1	Choose the best paraphrase of part of the passage or a sentence and analyze its meaning.

The other three question types found in the TOEFL® iBT are not multiple-choice and are types not found on older versions of the TOEFL®. One is a sentence insertion activity, and the last question can be one of two types of activities: either a summary question or a table/chart question.

Text Insertion Question

This question shows you a sentence that could be added to the passage. You must decide where the sentence would best fit in the passage. While you are reading, you will notice several icons that look like this ■ on the actual Internet-based test. You will be required to click on the square [■] where you feel the new sentence should be added. For the purposes of this book, simply choose the letter beside the appropriate square. This question tests how well you understand the organization of the passage, as well as grammatical connections between sentences.

Table/Chart Question

For passages on topics that explain groups or categories of information, you may be asked to demonstrate your understanding of the groups or categories mentioned by completing a chart. There will be two or three categories and either five or seven correct choices. Two of the answer choices will not be used. This question requires the ability to organize important information and to understand relationships between major ideas presented in the passage.

- **Example:**

Frogs	Toads
_____	_____
_____	_____
_____	_____
_____	

(A) bumpy, dry skin
(B) eggs in a chain
(C) build nests
(D) shorter legs
(E) eggs in a bunch
(F) have live babies
(G) longer legs
(H) smooth, wet skin
(I) bulging eyes

- **Correct answers:**

Frogs	Toads
eggs in a bunch	bumpy, dry skin
longer legs	eggs in a chain
smooth, wet skin	shorter legs
bulging eyes	

- **Not used:** build nests, have live babies

The chart questions are worth up to three points if there are five correct answers and four points if there are seven correct answers. Partial credit is awarded for having some but not all correct answers.

Summary Question

In this type of question, you will be presented with an introductory sentence for a brief summary of the passage. You will then find six additional sentences. Three of the sentences express major ideas in the passage, and the others do not. Incorrect choices will be either minor ideas or ideas that are not presented in the passage. This question measures your ability to recognize important ideas from the passage and distinguish them from minor ideas or ideas that are not in the passage.

- **Example:**
  First sentence of introduction:
  Animals in the desert have different ways to live with little water.
  ⇨ Camels can live for a long time without water.
  ⇨ Desert plants do not need much water.
  ⇨ Desert reptiles and birds do not sweat.
  ⇨ Larger animals get the water they need from things they eat.
  ⇨ At night, desert temperatures can drop below ten degrees Celsius.
  ⇨ Some animals stay underground to keep water in their skin.

- **Correct answers:**
  First sentence of introduction:
  Animals in the desert have different ways to live with little water.
  ⇨ Desert reptiles and birds do not sweat.
  ⇨ Larger animals get the water they need from things they eat.
  ⇨ Some animals stay underground to keep water in their skin.

- **Not used:**
  ⇨ Camels can live for a long time without water. (minor detail)
  ⇨ Desert plants do not need much water. (incorrect information)
  ⇨ At night, desert temperatures can drop below ten degrees Celsius. (minor detail)

The summary question is worth up to 2 points. Partial credit is awarded for having some but not all correct answers.

Study Tips for Reading

- Practice reading passages of academic English regularly (the Internet can be a great source of practice materials).

- Become a master of vocabulary and constructions:
  ⇨ Make it your goal to understand all the words you come across when studying.

- Keep a vocabulary notebook listing new terms and their definitions. Write out the definitions in English. Only refer to bilingual dictionaries if you cannot understand a word used in context or its definition from an English-only dictionary. Set aside a period of time every week to review your new vocabulary. Practice it by writing out your own sentences using the words.
- Master any and all grammatical and rhetorical constructions you encounter. Discover their meanings and uses by asking a teacher or doing an Internet search and viewing multiple examples of their use. You can keep a notebook of constructions as well.

- Learn how to take notes. You are permitted to take notes during the reading section of the TOEFL®. Note-taking is not writing down every word of the reading. A good idea is to note the main idea and then note the information that supports it. Note-taking must be learned, and it takes time. The better your note-taking skills, the easier you should find the TOEFL® reading section, as well as other sections of the TOEFL® iBT.

- Do not use a pencil or your finger when you are reading. Your eyes move faster than your finger, so you slow yourself down if you trace lines with a pencil or finger while reading.

Test Management

- Questions cannot be viewed until after the passage has been read.

- You will be allowed to study the reading as you answer the questions.

- Use the Review icon at the top of the screen to return to previous questions.

- There is a glossary available. Simply select the particular word with the cursor to find its meaning.

- When reading passages, ask yourself the following questions:
  - What is the main idea of the passage?
  - How is the main idea developed/supported in the passage?

- For each paragraph or new point in the passage, ask yourself why the author mentions it and how it relates to the main idea.

- Keep in mind that you have 60 to 100 minutes to read the passages and answer all of the questions in the reading section. This means that you can spend roughly 20 minutes on each set. Try to pace yourself accordingly. For each set, first answer the questions that you can answer easily. Then go back and answer more difficult questions. If you find that you have exceeded 20 minutes for a particular section, it is best to guess an answer and move on to the next section rather than remain on a particularly difficult question for several minutes

Preview Test

Directions

You will read one passage and then answer reading comprehension questions about it. Most questions are worth one point, but the last question is worth more than one point. The directions indicate how many points you may receive.

You will have 20 minutes to read the passage and answer the questions.

You may see a word or phrase in the passage that is underlined in blue. Definitions or explanations for these words or phrases are provided at the end of the passage.

You can skip questions and return to them later as long as there is time remaining.

When you are ready, press **Continue**.

Kelp and its Benefits

The ocean is an ecosystem that offers a bounty that humans have found invaluable for years. Thriving on the ocean floor is a form of seaweed, or alga, known as kelp. Kelp is a cold-water species, living primarily in the temperate and Arctic waters of the Northern Hemisphere. Kelp requires clear, shallow waters, since it relies on light for photosynthesis. In cold, nutrient-rich waters, the alga grows in underwater masses known as kelp forests, which offer a habitat for some ocean creatures and a food source for others. In the marine environment, they rank among the most biologically productive territories. This particular seaweed has a variety of purposes and has been utilized for centuries in the industrial and household realms. It plays a vital role in the balance of the ecosystem, affecting ocean life and human existence as well.

The appearance of kelp resembles that of a plant, but it is not classified as such. Kelp belongs to the Protista kingdom. Members of the Protista kingdom resemble fungi, plants, or animals, but share a relatively simple organization, being either unicellular or multi-cellular with unspecialized tissues. Kelp is similar to a plant, but has a simple, multi-cellular development. The structure of the alga consists of the holdfast, the stalk or stipe, and the fronds made up of long, leaf-like blades. The holdfast roots the seaweed to the ocean floor. Unlike plant roots that grow into the ground and gain nutrients from the soil, the holdfast attaches to the top of a rocky surface, anchoring the seaweed in place. Between the stipe and each blade is a gas bladder that supports the frond and keeps it afloat.

These unusual characteristics of kelp make it a valuable commodity to harvest. Humans gather the long, flat, broad leaves of the seaweed to use for production. In the past, harvesters would encircle a stand of kelp with a cable and pull on the cable to dislodge the alga from the rocky surface of the ocean floor. This method removed the whole plant, including the holdfast. Modern procedures only cut off the fronds of the plant, leaving the long-living holdfast intact and able to continue growing. The process involves barges equipped with blades that float on the ocean's surface into kelp forests. Their purpose is to gather the top of the alga without damaging the alga itself.

Harvested kelp, once it is processed, has multiple roles in the manufacturing field. Burning kelp is a common technique to process the alga once it is removed from its environment, and the product offers manifold functions. This kelp ash, or soda ash, is primarily sodium carbonate, and it is rich in iodine and alkali. Businesses worldwide reap the benefits of utilizing seaweed. Uses for iodine span the industrial spectrum, including pharmaceuticals, antiseptics, catalysts, food supplements, water purifiers, halogen lights, and photography. An alkali is a basic, ionic salt that dissolves in water and comes from alkaline earth metals. Components of gunpowder and lye soap are two of the numerous purposes for the alkali found in kelp.

Kelp's qualities extend beyond the inherent iodine and alkali elements. A kelp derivative called alginate is a carbohydrate used as a thickening substance in ice cream, jelly, toothpaste, and salad dressing. Another derivative of kelp is applied as an emulsifier to create a smooth texture in products such as processed foods, pharmaceuticals, paints, and cosmetics. In Japanese cuisine, an essential ingredient is kombu, one of several Pacific species of kelp. It is used as a garnish, a vegetable, and a flavoring for broth or porridge.

■ **A)** Scotland, Norway, China, and the US are now the primary producers of alga products, with smaller amounts contributed by Japan, Chile, France, and Spain. ■ **B)** Centuries ago, Scotland was the leading source of kelp ash production until the introduction of newer processes, beginning around the 1800s. ■ **C)** Production continues today. ■ **D)** However, despite kelp's natural abundance, a great deal of responsibility is required. Studies have shown that the number of kelp forests has decreased over the past several decades. After gathering kelp for centuries, harvesters must notice the effects of their labors on ocean life. Vital to human manufacturing as kelp has become, its original role in the environment is to provide essential food and habitat for ocean organisms as well as to keep the balance of the marine ecosystem it inhabits.

▸ **stand**
   a group of several plants growing together in one place

▸ **barge**
   a long, flat boat

▸ **emulsifier**
   a substance added to food to prevent liquid and solid parts from separating

---

1. According to paragraph 1, which of the following characteristics is unique to a kelp forest?

(A) It grows in all types of ocean water.
(B) It requires deep water to reach its growth potential.
(C) It needs water with nutrients for food.
(D) It grows in clear waters within the reach of light.

2. Which of the following can be inferred from paragraph 1 about kelp?

(A) Kelp forests do not support much marine life.
(B) Kelp does not grow in warm equatorial waters.
(C) Kelp requires a lot of prey to survive.
(D) The waters of Antarctica provide a suitable habitat for kelp.

3. According to paragraph 2, what is true about the individual structure of kelp?

   (A) The holdfast makes up the leafy, larger portion of the organism.
   (B) The gas bladders are essential in keeping kelp upright.
   (C) The root is secured on the ocean floor, allowing the fronds to float freely.
   (D) The stipe serves as the main support for kelp's structure.

4. The word encircle in the passage is closest in meaning to

   (A) surround
   (B) hide
   (C) capture
   (D) extract

5. Which of the following can be inferred from paragraph 3 about harvesting kelp?

   (A) Kelp can survive if the holdfast is not destroyed.
   (B) Modern harvesting procedures destroy lots of kelp.
   (C) Harvesters used to gather the holdfasts for use in production.
   (D) Harvesting kelp is a new process that is still changing.

6. The author discusses harvesting techniques in paragraph 3 in order to

   (A) offer instructions on how to gather kelp
   (B) show improvements in gathering methods
   (C) describe the nature of kelp that is gathered
   (D) introduce the process of involving barges

7. The word Their in the passage refers to

   (A) Algae
   (B) Procedures
   (C) Barges
   (D) Rocky surfaces

8. The word manifold in the passage is closest in meaning to

   (A) extreme
   (B) limited
   (C) multiple
   (D) specific

9. All of the following are mentioned in paragraph 4 as uses of kelp-derived iodine EXCEPT:

   (A) Creating weapons
   (B) Purifying water
   (C) Cleaning wounds
   (D) Improving food

10. The word derivative in the passage is closest in meaning to

    (A) impact
    (B) replica
    (C) product
    (D) additive

11. According to paragraph 5, alginate serves as

    (A) a substance used to create paint
    (B) a popular garnish for certain foods
    (C) an element used in manufacturing kelp
    (D) a thickener for gel-like substances

12. Look at the four squares [■] that indicate where the following sentence could be added to the passage.

These methods, coupled with the economic collapse of the Scottish kelp industry, paved the way for other countries to begin producing kelp on a large-scale.

Where would the sentence best fit?

(A) First square
(B) Second square
(C) Third square
(D) Fourth square

13. Which of the sentences below best expresses the essential information in the highlighted sentence? Incorrect choices change the meaning in important ways or leave out essential information.

(A) Kelp plays a major role in the marine environment and in industry.
(B) Kelp has grown increasingly important in manufacturing.
(C) Kelp keeps its ecosystem and the surrounding marine life in balance.
(D) Kelp is best left in its native environment because of over-harvesting.

14. Directions: An introductory sentence for a brief summary of the passage is provided below. Complete the summary by selecting the THREE answer choices that express the most important ideas in the passage. Some answer choices do not belong in the summary because they express ideas that are not presented in the passage or are minor ideas in the passage. *This question is worth 2 points.*

Ocean kelp has an important place in the ecosystem and offers many benefits to humans.

-
-
-

Answer Choices

(A) Kelp is vital to marine life because it offers homes and food to sea dwellers.
(B) Soda ash, which is primarily sodium carbonate, yields iodine and alkali.
(C) Kelp products are used in a number of manufacturing processes and goods.
(D) Groups of kelp exist as kelp forests and require cool, shallow water to survive.
(E) Raw or cooked kelp can be used as either a garnish or a vegetable.
(F) Kelp harvesting has continued for centuries as humans realized its many uses.

Chapter 1 Fact Questions

Necessary Skills

- Identifying important information and facts stated in a passage
- Locating a specific piece of information in a passage quickly
- Understanding the distinction between main ideas and supporting details
- Focusing on facts, details, definitions, or other information presented in a passage

Example Questions

- According to the passage, who/when/where/what/how/why _____?
- According to paragraph X, which of the following is true of _____?
- The author's description of _____ mentions which of the following?
- According to paragraph X, _____ occurred because _____
- According to the passage, why did X do Y?

Strategies

- Look for transitional expressions to locate details such as examples, steps, time, reasons, or results.
- Pay attention to examples and descriptions that provide information and details.
- Eliminate choices presenting information that contradicts what is provided in the passage.
- Answer the specific question being asked. Do not select an answer just because it is mentioned in the passage.

01 Linguistics

ngôn ngữ học

Read the following passage. Then fill in the diagram with the information that you read. `Track 2`

biểu đồ

English and the Gold Rush

The discovery of gold in California in 1848 marked the beginning of an economic boom known as the California Gold Rush. The miners, many of whom were originally journalists, lawyers, and businessmen, preserved their experiences in writing. Much of this was peppered with colorful phrases related to their new work. Interestingly, many of these phrases are still in use today in the English language.

The popular phrase "pan out," meaning "to be successful," can be traced back to the gold rush. Miners would separate gold from worthless minerals using a pan; gold would settle to the bottom of the pan, and other sediments would be removed. The likely origin of "pan out," then, is from the process of gathering all the gold in one's pan.

In addition, the phrase "strike it rich" originated from the Gold Rush. This phrase has come to mean "to become wealthy quickly." A strike is literally a discovery, in this case, of gold. During the Gold Rush, if a miner "struck it rich," he found gold and thus became wealthy. Having lost its original meaning, the same phrase is used today when people make money quickly in business or win a lottery.

mark:
to be a defining feature of

boom:
a rapid increase

pepper:
to fill with lots of examples of something

trace:
to follow or be followed

settle:
to come to rest

sediment:
material that settles to the bottom of water

The Effect of the Gold Rush on the English Language

Theory:	Example 1:
	Example 2:

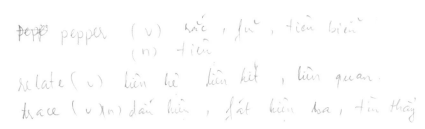

1. Which of the following is true according to paragraph 1?

   (A) Introducing new phrases into English was the goal of the writers.
   (B) Not all of the Gold Rush miners could read or write.
   (C) The miners wrote about their gold-mining experiences.
   (D) Miners preferred their lives as journalists, lawyers, and businessmen.

2. According to paragraph 2, where did the phrase "pan out" originate?

   (A) Miners called their findings "pans."
   (B) Miners used pans to find their gold.
   (C) Gold was found in places called pans.
   (D) Miners called selling gold "panning."

3. According to paragraph 3, what does "strike it rich" mean today?

   (A) To find gold
   (B) To break a rock apart
   (C) To lose one's wealth
   (D) To get money fast

Fill in the blanks to complete the summary.

The passage discusses English phrases that can be ____traced____ back to the gold rush in California. The phrase "pan out" came from the pans that miners used. Gold would ____settle____ to the bottom of their pans, and the ____sediment____ would be removed. The expression "____strike____ it rich" originated from miners striking the rocks to find gold and becoming ____wealthy____ quickly if they found it.

02 Theater

Read the following passage. Then fill in the diagram with the information that you read. `Track 3`

The Greek Chorus and the Audience

In Greek theater, the chorus was either a person or a group of people that served various purposes in supporting the play. It provided a commentary on the play by emphasizing the major themes and by clarifying the plot. The chorus also influenced reactions of the audience by engaging in overt communication with it.

To help the audience understand the events, the chorus helped to reinforce the main points of the play. It often revealed background information that the characters could not deliver—such as inner emotions like fear and resentment—without needlessly interrupting the play. Through either singing or speaking in unison, the chorus conveyed ideas that characters were unable to say. Also, an overview of events was sometimes presented to the audience members to facilitate their interpretation of the story. This would improve understanding and enhance enjoyment of the play.

Finally, the chorus could sway audience responses by displaying embellished reactions to prompt the audience to react similarly. Likewise, laugh tracks today can prompt television viewers to laugh. Another way the chorus interacted with the audience was by discussing events and characters. This was achieved by either mocking or sympathizing with them. This clever tool to influence feelings and reactions of the audience altered the dynamic between the audience and the play itself.

clarify:
to free from confusion

commentary:
an explanation or illustration of something

overt:
explicit or easily seen or recognized

reinforce:
to emphasize

unison:
in harmony; at the same time

facilitate:
to make easier

embellish:
to exaggerate

laugh track:
a pre-recorded segment of laughter that is added to a TV or radio program to mimic audience responses

The Greek Chorus and the Audience

Definition:

Role 1:

Role 2:

- convey (v) thuyền đạt, chuyển, sáng tên
- character (n) đặc tích, đặc điểm, cá tích, đặc trưng
- overview (n) tổng quan, khái quát, ngắn gọn
- present (a) có mặt, hiện diện
  (n) quà tặng   (v) bày tỏ, biểu thị

1. According to paragraph 1, what was the role of the chorus in Greek theater?

  (A) To introduce new characters
  (B) To provide music for the play
  (C) To analyze the audience's reactions
  (D) To help the audience understand

3. According to paragraph 3, why did the chorus present overstated emotions?

  (A) To parody the play's characters
  (B) To encourage audience reactions
  (C) To explain important events
  (D) To provide new information

- facilitate (v) tạo đắc thuận lợi, dễ dàng
- interpretation (n) sự giải thích, làm sáng tỏ, phiên dịch, cắt nghĩa
- enhance (v) nâng cao, đề cao, nổi bật, gia tăng, tăng

2. According to paragraph 2, how did the chorus communicate characters' emotions?

  (A) By telling the audience how to react
  (B) By summarizing the play after it ended
  (C) By presenting the thoughts of the characters
  (D) By repeating their thoughts during the play

- sway (v) gây a.h, ảnh hưởng (n) sự tác động, tác động
- response (n) sự trả lời, hưởng ứng, đáp trả
- embellish (v) làm đẹp, trang điểm, thêm thắt, thêm màu thêm mỡ (vào 1 chuyện...)

Fill in the blanks to complete the summary.

The role of the chorus in Greek theater was to provide a(n) _____ on a play to the audience in order to _____ the plot. The chorus explained the stories and _____ the audience's understanding of events. By singing or speaking in _____, the chorus was also responsible for influencing the way audiences reacted to a play. It did this by showing _____ reactions and discussing the play's events and characters with the audience.

- chorus (n) bài hát đồng thanh, hợp ca
- commentary (n) bài bút luận / tường thuật / lời dẫn giải
- emphasize (v) nhấn mạnh
- major (n) chuyên đề (a) lớn, trọng đại
- theme (n) đề tài, chủ đề
- clarify (v) bóc ngắn, làm trong
- plot (n) miêu đất nhỏ / cốt truyện
- influence (n) sự ảnh, tác dụng (v) sự tác / thúc
- reaction (n) sự pư lại, sự tác pư
- communication (n) sự truyền đạt / liên lạc

- engage (v) thu hút, hứa hẹn, cam kết
- reinforce (v) củng cố, tăng cường, nhấn mạnh
- reveal (v) bộc lộ, biểu lộ, phát hiện
- inner (a) nội bộ, thân cận, (n)
- emotion (n) cảm xúc, cảm động
- resentment (n) sự oán giận
- needlessly thừa, vô ích
- unison (n) giọng đồng thanh, nhất trí

03 Ecology

Read the following passage. Then fill in the diagram with the information that you read. `Track 4`

Effects of Global Warming on Coral Reefs

Global warming is contributing to the shift in weather patterns across the globe, causing higher air temperatures. In turn, the warmer air alters the temperatures of the oceans and causes significant changes to the world's ecosystems. In particular, coral reefs, considered one of the most vulnerable ecosystems with regard to temperature changes, could be destroyed forever.

Coral is a brightly colored sea animal that can only thrive in a limited temperature range. When the water rises above the coral's temperature threshold for a prolonged period of time, the coral is damaged. While this temperature threshold differs between different types of coral, they generally cannot survive in waters above thirty degrees Celsius. If the ocean water gets too warm, coral goes through a process of bleaching, in which it loses the algae that give coral its vibrant colors. Bleaching is an indication of damage to the coral. While it is possible to survive the damage, most corals do not. In the western region of the Indian Ocean, rising temperatures have contributed to bleaching in an estimated ninety percent of native corals.

In addition, changes in weather patterns due to global warming have contributed to an increase in tropical storms. The choppy waves damage coral reefs. Also, the rain can cause flooding on land. When overflowing rivers deposit their runoff into the ocean, the incoming sediment clouds the water with tiny particles. These particles act as a screen that blocks the passage of sunlight. Since the algae that live within the coral depend upon photosynthesis to live, the decrease in available sunlight limits their ability to undergo this process. Without adequate sunlight, the algae die, and therefore, so do the corals.

alter:
to change or modify

ecosystem:
the sum of the organisms in an environment

vulnerable:
not protected; defenseless

temperature threshold:
the highest or lowest temperature at which an organism can live

indication:
a sign; a characteristic

prolonged:
continued; constant

runoff:
material that is drained off, such as from a river

cloud:
to make less clear

Changes in Coral Reefs

Cause 1:

Effect:

Cause 2:

Effect:

1. According to paragraph 2, how does ocean temperature damage coral?

   (A) By breaking pieces off of coral
   (B) By bleaching coral reefs
   (C) By killing coral's food source
   (D) By introducing harmful sediment

2. According to paragraph 2, what is bleaching?

   (A) The loss of algae in coral reefs
   (B) The temperature threshold for coral
   (C) The loss of color in coral reefs
   (D) The ability for coral to survive

3. According to paragraph 3, what effect does sediment have on coral?

   (A) It covers the algae and causes it to break.
   (B) It makes the water warmer and kills the coral.
   (C) It increases the water pressure and breaks coral reefs.
   (D) It prevents the algae from receiving enough sunlight.

Fill in the blanks to complete the summary.

Global warming is responsible for _____ the ocean's temperatures, which affects coral reefs. Coral reefs are _____ to temperature changes, and they become damaged if exposed to higher temperatures for _____ periods. One _____ of coral damage due to warm ocean temperatures is bleaching. An increase in tropical storms is another way coral reefs are being damaged because of global warming. Sediment from overflowing rivers _____ the ocean, which decreases the amount of sunlight reaching the corals.

---

04 Literature

Read the following passage. Then fill in the diagram with the information that you read. `Track 5`

The Ascent of the Novel

The novel was first defined as any long narrative prose that portrayed aspects of everyday life through fictional characters and events. The novel appeared during the time that romance was popular. The invention of Gutenberg's printing press in 1429 significantly increased the literacy rate and the production and distribution of written texts. Both the romance and the novel flourished during this time, though they were very different in content and style.

The novel included different types of characters than those found in romance stories. The latter described entertaining adventures about heroes with the purpose of relating moral teachings. Often, knights were the main heroes of romances, as in the 14th-century tale *Sir Gawain and the Green Knight*. The main theme of the story was the glories of knighthood. The novel, on the other hand, featured daily events and ordinary people. The novel often parodied romance's typical style of impossible, glorified characters. The romance genre was favored by the nobility, who enjoyed the formal language and found it perfectly appropriate for describing the deeds of heroes. In contrast, the prose used in novels was considered "low," and thus more appropriate for satire.

Yet another difference was that the novel represented human existence in a way that was closer to real life and included few exaggerations. It portrayed the human experience through events with which the average reader could identify. This allowed an opportunity to engage in a study of human character. In contrast, romance stories presented a colorful distortion of the characteristics and lives of people through idealism. Through the novel, one could learn about the real motives and temperaments of people in a generally realistic way. With a romance, the point of emphasis is plot, while a novel's main focal point is character. For example, Daniel Defoe's *Robinson Crusoe*, considered to be one of the first "modern" novels, was told in first-person narrative, through which the reader becomes intimately familiar with the main character.

prose:
the ordinary form of written or spoken language

distribution:
the giving out of things

flourish:
to be successful

parody:
to imitate someone or something comically

satire:
a genre that uses irony, sarcasm, and ridicule

temperament:
a range of moods or personality fluctuations

focal:
related to the center of attention

| The Romance vs. The Novel | | |

The Romance	Both	The Novel
• • •	•	• • •

1. According to paragraph 2, what was the purpose of romance stories?

   (A) To teach morals through adventurous tales
   (B) To show characters who were unrealistic
   (C) To educate the public about knighthood
   (D) To demonstrate typical daily life

2. According to paragraph 3, how did the novel portray characters?

   (A) As exciting and heroic
   (B) Idealistically
   (C) As honest and tender
   (D) Realistically

3. According to paragraph 3, which is true of romance stories?

   (A) They tend to show people's problems and faults.
   (B) They have highly developed plot structures.
   (C) They emphasize a character's effect upon the plot.
   (D) Their plots can be formed with common situations.

Fill in the blanks to complete the summary.

The passage discusses the appearance of the novel as it _____ along with the romance in the 15ᵗʰ century. The invention of the printing press increased the _____ of written texts to people. The novel often _____ the impossible characters and formal style of the romance, instead presenting more realistic _____ and motives of people. Also, the main _____ point of the novel was character, as opposed to plot in the romance.

05 | Anthropology

Read the following passage. Then fill in the diagram with the information that you read. `Track 6`

Symbolic Behavior

People throughout history have developed ways to cope with uncertainty in life. Symbolic behavior, which can be defined as any superstitious action that attempts to bring about a supernatural result, is one way that people have dealt with uncertainty. A recent poll showed that over half of Americans hold some superstitious beliefs, even if they know that they are illogical. Nonetheless, superstitions may have positive psychological effects. Both rituals and taboos—two common types of symbolic behavior—can help reduce anxiety and give a person a sense of control.

Rituals involve any behavior that is done repeatedly in order to produce a desired outcome. Generally, rituals express a person's anxiety symbolically. This means the behavior is an attempt to lead to a result through an unrelated action. Those who believe in the power of rituals often feel that breaking the ritual will produce negative consequences, perhaps even supernatural punishment. Psychologically, ritualistic behavior can provide a sense of control over often uncontrollable situations. For instance, Wayne Gretzky, a Hall-of-Fame hockey player, tucked in his jersey in the exact same manner before each game. The outcome of a hockey game obviously cannot be controlled solely by a single hockey player. However, a ritual may give a player the feeling that he has control over the team's success, even if it is through the superstitious habit of putting on a jersey in a certain way.

Some people do certain things like perform rituals to obtain the help of the supernatural. Others do *not* do certain things for the same reason. A taboo is a forbidden behavior. Taboos can reduce anxiety in a number of situations through what a person does not do. Taboos often originate from beliefs that if a certain action is performed (often in a particular context), some tragedy or misfortune will transpire. Unlike ritual, taboo does not involve repetition. Even one incidence of the tabooed behavior may result in supernatural punishment. This type of symbolic behavior can be seen in the habits of New England fishermen. These fishermen have many taboos while at sea, such as whistling on board or saying the word "pig." Although even the fishermen themselves admit that they do not believe the taboos have any effect, they continue to follow them. In essence, these taboos assure the fishermen that they are doing everything that they can to avoid misfortune. As a result, they are able to set out to sea with a more positive mindset.

cope:
to deal with emotionally

symbolic:
representing something that cannot otherwise be expressed

outcome:
a result

jersey:
a shirt worn as part of a sports uniform

solely:
alone; as the only influence

transpire:
to occur

Symbolic Behavior

Theory:		Support 1:
	→	Support 2:

1. According to paragraph 1, how are rituals and taboos related?
   (A) They both require that an action be performed.
   (B) They are known to ease one's level of stress.
   (C) A taboo can often result from ritualistic behavior.
   (D) Written symbols can be included in both behaviors.

2. According to paragraph 2, why is a ritual said to be symbolic?
   (A) Because it connects actions that are not related
   (B) Because breaking the ritual will cause problems

   (C) Because it involves perceptions of supernatural powers
   (D) Because it gives people control over their lives

3. Which of the following is true according to paragraph 3?
   (A) Taboos cause people to fear breaking ritualistic behaviors.
   (B) Fishermen believe that taboos protect them from the supernatural.
   (C) People may follow a taboo while claiming not to believe in it.
   (D) People believe more in taboos after a tragedy occurs.

Fill in the blanks to complete the summary.

The passage discusses symbolic behavior as a means for people to _____ with uncertainty in their lives. Two common types of _____ behavior are rituals and taboos. Rituals are behaviors done repeatedly in order to bring about a certain _____. Although a ritual cannot _____ bring about a desired result, an individual can get a feeling of control through performing the ritual. Taboos are forbidden behaviors that can make some people believe that something terrible will _____. By avoiding a certain taboo, a person may feel that he or she can also avoid misfortune.

06 Sociology

Read the following passage. Then fill in the diagram with the information that you read. `Track 7`

The Dutch East India Company

Globalization is a process of integration. It began centuries ago and continues to develop today. It can be defined as the internationalization of political, economic, cultural, and social systems. Perhaps the most significant example of the early rise of global culture is the Dutch East India Company. Established in 1602 by the Dutch, who were then colonizing the East Indies of the Indian Ocean, it was the world's first multinational corporation. The Dutch East India Company was a key impetus in the trend of globalization, in that it significantly changed export activity and created an avenue for extensive cultural exchange.

There was strong competition in the world market for trade amongst the European nations. One by one, they moved across the seas in order to expand their empires. The best way they could assert their power in the growing world was through economic expansion. The Dutch happened to emerge as a powerful entity mostly through their maritime trade capabilities and were therefore able to establish their empire in the Orient. As the Dutch trade grew, so too did its economic power. Silver and copper were brought from Peru and Japan to trade with India and China for various textiles such as silk and cotton. Those items were then traded with other Asian nations for spices such as cinnamon and pepper, which were in great demand in Europe.

The company's trade activity also contributed to the spread of culture. The Dutch government had granted the company a monopoly over the trade of the "Spice Islands" of the East Indies. Not only did it enter into trade agreements with the sovereign rulers of the nations of the East Indies, but it also saw its competition reduced. This rise in power came when the Dutch government expelled the Portuguese and British from Indonesia and Sri Lanka. The company even collaborated with missionaries, and through them was able to trade new cultural items with Japan and China. In fact, though Japan closed itself to trade between 1640 and 1854, the company was the only trade group to have access to Japan. Thus, it was able to transport the Japanese kimono to Europe, where it became highly popular. Because of the route that was established through the Dutch East India Company, the cultural influences from each country circulated around the world. Traders along each stop were able to gain a broader base of knowledge about others involved in worldwide trade.

integration:
the combination of parts into a whole

impetus:
a moving force or stimulus

avenue:
a path

expel:
to drive out or send away

collaborate:
to work together

circulate:
to move from place to place

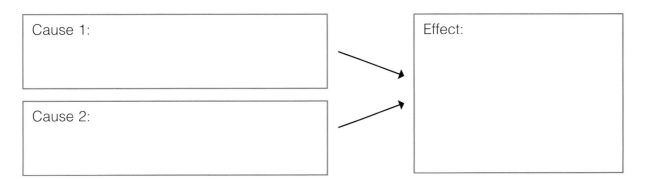

1. According to paragraph 1, what event occurred at the same time that the Dutch East India Company was established?

   (A) The colonization of parts of Asia
   (B) The expansion of the Dutch government
   (C) The increase of the spice trade within Asia
   (D) An increased need for inexpensive goods

2. According to paragraph 2, how did the Dutch East India Company gain economic power?

   (A) Through its ability to trade extensively at sea
   (B) By increasing its reliance upon Dutch funding

   (C) By receiving help from the Dutch military
   (D) By refusing to trade with other western countries

3. According to paragraph 3, how did missionaries affect trade?

   (A) They aided in expelling the British from the East Indies.
   (B) They allowed clothing to be transported to Europe.
   (C) They aided the Dutch government's military.
   (D) They helped the Dutch to establish a trade monopoly.

Fill in the blanks to complete the summary.

The passage discusses the Dutch East India Company as an important _____ in the trend of globalization beginning in the 17th century. It provided a(n) _____ for cultural exchanges through the trade of goods by sea. Through their _____ trade abilities, the Dutch grew in power and eliminated competition by _____ the Portuguese and the British from the East Indies. Through the trade activities of the Dutch East India Company, highly prized and exotic items such as spice and textiles were able to _____ around the world.

Chapter 2 — Negative Fact Questions

Necessary Skills

- Recognizing incorrect information as well as information not mentioned in the passage
- Identifying paraphrases that do or do not correctly summarize information from the passage
- Verifying that three answer choices are true and one is false

Example Questions

- All of the following are mentioned in paragraph X as _____ EXCEPT:
- According to the passage, which of the following is NOT _____?
- The author's description of _____ mentions all of the following EXCEPT:

Strategies

- Be aware that often, the three incorrect answer choices are spread across a paragraph or several paragraphs.
- Keep in mind that the correct answer either directly contradicts one or more statements in the passage or it is not mentioned in the passage at all.
- Check your answer to make sure that you understood the question accurately.

01 Psychology

Read the following passage. Then fill in the diagram with the information that you read. `Track 8`

Male and Female Conversations

The goal of social conversations is typically the same. Being friendly, showing concern for others, and talking about topics of interest are all typical aims for any conversation. However, when engaged in same-sex conversations, the ways in which women and men achieve these goals are remarkably different.

Men are far more likely to try to make conversation fun. This fact is seen in the high incidence of joking by men in same-sex conversations. Indeed, studies reveal that men are far more likely than women to include joking and innocent teasing in their conversations. The subject of personal feelings is seen as a sign of vulnerability and is therefore broached very infrequently. Further, men do not seem as inclined to call and chat as women do. Forty percent of the men polled in a recent survey said that they never call their same-sex friends "just to talk."

In contrast, women's same-sex conversations include more reference to feelings, relationships, and personal problems. Some psychologists have theorized that talk is essential to maintaining and nurturing female relationships. In maintaining their relationships, women tend to engage in more frequent conversations with their same-sex friends. In fact, almost half of the women in a recent survey stated that they called their female friends on a weekly basis just to chat.

engaged:
busy with a task

incidence:
the rate at which something occurs

innocent:
harmless

vulnerability:
the state of being exposed

broach:
to mention

nurture:
to support

Conversation: Men vs. Women

Men	Both	Women
•	•	•
•		•

1. According to paragraphs 1 and 2, all of the following are true of conversation EXCEPT:

   (A) Most people converse for very similar reasons.
   (B) Men and women converse in different ways.
   (C) Men often tease women while talking to them.
   (D) Men do not typically like to discuss emotions.

2. The author's description of male conversation mentions all of the following EXCEPT:

   (A) Men generally try to use conversation for amusement.
   (B) Men sometimes hurt others through teasing.
   (C) Men feel that discussing feelings makes them appear weak.
   (D) Many men see emotion as a sign of weakness.

3. According to paragraph 3, which of the following is NOT true of women's conversations?

   (A) Women often discuss personal relationships.
   (B) Conversations are essential to female friendships.
   (C) Many females call their friends regularly.
   (D) Most women fear discussing their emotions.

Fill in the blanks to complete the summary.

According to the passage, men and women _____ in very different same-sex conversations. For men, talk is generally not personal, is more likely to include _____ teasing and joking, and is not very common. Men often consider personal feelings a sign of _____. By contrast, women often _____ personal topics such as feelings and problems with one another. Female conversation is thought to be very important to maintain and _____ female relationships.

---

02 Agriculture

Read the following passage. Then fill in the diagram with the information that you read. `Track 9`

Shortage of Water Resources

The lack of clean, suitable water for agricultural purposes is a growing global problem. One of the best ways to counter this problem is to ensure that water is used more efficiently. Since agriculture is the greatest user of water, it is of great importance that farmers and agronomists alike seek out ways to increase the efficiency of irrigation.

A simple method of water conservation is already being used in many countries: sub-surface irrigation. When irrigation systems apply water above the surface of the ground, much of that water either evaporates or runs off. In warm climates, this waste has been estimated at nearly fifty percent. In other words, half of all the water applied is lost. In sub-surface irrigation, as the name implies, water is introduced below the surface of the ground. This action significantly reduces water loss. Not only is water saved, but the more uniform application of water to the plants' root systems leads to hardier plants with more abundant yields.

Another novel way to use water more efficiently is to grow crops that are native to the region. Because species have adapted over time to their native regions, they are often able to handle local conditions better than non-native species. Corn, native to parts of Mexico, is an example of how native species can reduce the need for significant irrigation. In the latter decades of the 20th century, non-native species of corn from the United States were introduced to and sold in Mexico. While farmers enjoyed significant yields from these introduced species, their water usage skyrocketed. This resulted in water-table depletion throughout many agricultural regions in Mexico. In response, Mexican farmers have recently reintroduced native corn species that are better able to handle arid climates.

counter:
to oppose; to express an opposite view

agronomist:
one who studies soil and crops

evaporate:
to convert a liquid into a gas

uniform:
consistent

hardier:
stronger

novel:
new

depletion:
the act of reducing the supply of something

Water Shortage

Problem:

Solution 1:

Solution 2:

1. According to paragraph 1, which of the following is NOT true of the water shortage?

   (A) It is a problem that occurs all around the world.
   (B) It can be countered by using water more efficiently.
   (C) It is caused partially by farming practices.
   (D) It is affecting worldwide drinking water supplies.

3. According to paragraph 3, which is NOT true?

   (A) Plant species can adapt to their environments.
   (B) Non-native corn in Mexico requires increased watering.
   (C) Mexican farmers are now using more native corn species.
   (D) Mexican corn produces higher yields than US corn.

2. Based upon information in paragraph 2, all of the following are true EXCEPT:

   (A) An above-ground system is less efficient than a sub-surface system.
   (B) Underground irrigation reduces evaporation and runoff.
   (C) Crop yields improve when underground irrigation is used fifty percent of the time.
   (D) A sub-surface irrigation system gives water directly to the roots.

Fill in the blanks to complete the summary.

The passage discusses ways in which farmers are trying to _____ shortages of clean, fresh water. When crops are watered above the surface of the ground, much of the water _____ instead of reaching the plants. By installing new underground irrigation systems, a more _____ application of water can reach the root systems of the plants. Another _____ idea for farmers to use water more efficiently is to grow more native species of crops. Native crops can grow without excessive watering, thus slowing the _____ of precious water resources.

---

03 Marketing

Read the following passage. Then fill in the diagram with the information that you read. `Track 10`

Product Demonstration

Marketers have long advertised their products in newspapers, magazines, and on the radio. Given the billions of dollars spent on these forms each year, they must certainly be useful. Yet as advantageous as such advertising is, there is perhaps no better way to sell a product than by offering a hands-on demonstration of it. Doing so allows the potential customer, depending on the product, to touch, drive, or taste it.

One of the main benefits of product demonstration is that it makes the product more tangible to buyers. Until most consumers actually touch a product, it is nothing more than an advertisement in a magazine or on television. This is certainly the case with new-car sales in the United States. There, it is common for car shoppers to take a "test drive" of the vehicle that they are considering buying before making the actual purchase. It has been shown that car salespeople are very likely (some estimates put the likelihood at ninety percent) to offer a prospective customer a test drive within just five minutes of meeting that customer. There is, of course, a valid reason for this. Empirical studies show a test drive can increase the likelihood of a purchase significantly.

Another benefit of product demonstration is that it can make a product's selling points immediately apparent. This makes the product more appealing in the eyes of the potential customer. While print ads can certainly list these selling points, customers often want to see a product in use before they make the decision to purchase it. To illustrate, consider the situation faced by a leading manufacturer of non-stick cookware in the 1970s. The manufacturer had just created a substance that, when permanently applied to pots and pans, allowed cooked foods to separate easily from the cookware rather than stick, as was common with previous cookware. Initial consumer response to the product was very low. However, after demonstrating the non-stick substance's function at fairs and expositions, sales of the cookware soared.

advantageous:
beneficial; favorable

hands-on:
involving human participation

tangible:
real

prospective:
possible

empirical:
performed through experience or experiments

exposition:
a large public show

Product Demonstration

| Definition: | Advantage 1: | Example: |
| Advantage 2: | Example: |

1. According to paragraph 1, all of the following are true about product demonstrations EXCEPT:
   (A) They allow consumers to see how a product works.
   (B) They make customers more likely to purchase a product.
   (C) They display a product more effectively than a commercial.
   (D) They can be used through various forms of print advertisement.

2. Which of the following is NOT true according to paragraph 2?
   (A) Demonstrations can make a product seem real.
   (B) Vehicle test drives often increase car sales.
   (C) Car dealers often offer test drives to customers.
   (D) Over ninety percent of car customers take a test drive.

3. According to paragraph 3, all of the following are true EXCEPT:
   (A) Demonstrations can change a customer's opinion of a product.
   (B) Demonstrations work best after customers have seen a print ad first.
   (C) Many customers do not buy a product until they have seen it used.
   (D) A cookware company increased sales with product demonstrations.

Fill in the blanks to complete the summary.

According to the passage, while product advertising is _____ in selling goods and services, a hands-on demonstration is often more effective with _____ customers. Product demonstration makes an item more _____ to buyers, in that they can actually touch and use it before they buy it. This shows _____ what a product's function is, which can lead to higher sales of the product. For example, a manufacturer of non-stick cookware made many more sales after demonstrating its product at a(n) _____.

---

04 Political Science

Read the following passage. Then fill in the diagram with the information that you read. `Track 11`

Dependency Theory

Dependency theory originated in the 1950s to explain why certain nations remained poor and failed to integrate into the world economy. Even then, the world economy was becoming more global in scope. Poor nations today are still often dependent upon larger, more developed nations of the world. The theory states that they will remain so unless they enact major economic reform.

Dependency theory asserts that the economic development of poor nations cannot continue unless they significantly restructure their import and export programs. Raul Prebisch, a leading dependency theorist of the 1950s, stated that developing nations typically rely upon the export of raw materials or simple commodities for their economic well-being. Neither of these exports, however, can supply enough capital for these nations to expand their economies significantly. Further, these developing countries also import many of their basic needs, such as clothing, vehicles, and medicine. Prebisch noted that, in most developing countries, export activity is lower than import activity. Therefore, the revenue gained from exporting is considerably lower than the expenditures required to import such necessities. This reliance upon imports assures that developing nations cannot support a healthy economy.

An example of this theory was seen in many Caribbean nations. Countries in the Caribbean display economic dependence through their reliance on single exports (such as sugar) or industries (such as tourism). These countries rely on imports in order to fulfill their basic needs. For example, Grenada exports mainly bananas, cocoa, and nutmeg, since these grow well there. However, it imports machinery, fuel, manufactured goods, and many food items. The profits from the few export industries cannot match the necessary spending for imports. Therefore, Prebisch would argue, Grenada cannot progress economically and will remain dependent upon developed nations. Prebisch and other dependency theorists suggest that the only viable solution for these developing nations is to reduce dependency upon imports from other nations. To achieve this, the dependent countries must increase their level of manufacturing.

integrate:
to combine into a whole

restructure:
to change completely

capital:
money

revenue:
an amount of money brought in from sales

expenditure:
an amount spent; a cost

viable:
able to be put into practice; practical

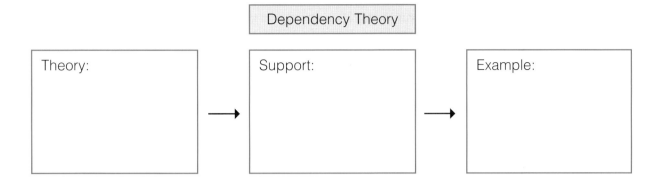

1. According to paragraph 1, all of the following are true of dependency theory EXCEPT:
   (A) It was introduced in the 1950s.
   (B) It explains why some nations remain poor.
   (C) It says that poor countries cannot progress.
   (D) It claims that small nations are dependent on developed nations.

2. Which of the following is NOT true about dependency theory according to the passage?
   (A) Developing nations do not gain revenue.
   (B) Developing nations must import less.

   (C) Developing nations often import more than they export.
   (D) Developing nations get many needs from other countries.

3. According to paragraph 3, which of the following is NOT true?
   (A) Reliance on a single export or import may be profitable.
   (B) Many Caribbean nations are dependent on other nations.
   (C) Imports must provide for the basic needs of Grenada.
   (D) Grenada spends more on imports than it gains on exports.

Fill in the blanks to complete the summary.

The passage discusses dependency theory, which explains why some developing nations cannot _____ into the world economy. These countries will not succeed economically until they _____ their import and export programs. Because the _____ gained from exports is much lower than the _____ needed to import basic goods, these nations cannot generate a healthy economy. Dependency theorists suggest that the only _____ solution for these countries is to increase manufacturing in order to decrease dependence upon developed nations for their welfare.

----

05 Anthropology

Read the following passage. Then fill in the diagram with the information that you read. `Track 12`

Ethnocentrism and Cultural Relativity

Ethnocentrism is defined as the interpretation of a culture based upon the standards of one's own culture. Cultural relativity, on the other hand, seeks to interpret a culture based solely upon that culture's standards. This is done with no attention given to other cultures. Increasingly, cultural relativity is the preferred means of cultural interpretation for anthropologists.

Ethnocentrism is common both as a social and an anthropological means of interpretation. Generally, ethnocentrism is a universal phenomenon. For example, ethnocentrism can be seen in something as simple as an American citizen stating that the English drive on the "wrong" side of the road. By stating that the other side is wrong, this hypothetical citizen has judged another culture based upon that of the United States.

This becomes a more serious issue in anthropology when it affects the way entire cultures are represented. One well-known researcher accused of an ethnocentric view is Erich von Däniken, a Swiss author and archaeologist. Through his studies, von Däniken concluded that many historical societies, such as the ancient Egyptians, were not as advanced as other cultures. Therefore, he speculated, they could not have completed the Great Pyramids without assistance. This assistance, von Däniken claims, must have come from extraterrestrial beings.

Cultural relativism, on the other hand, essentially reverses the thought process of ethnocentrism. Thus, cultural judgments are based on the realization that there is no universal standard for culture. Cultures are distinctive and equal in terms of value—a position many find difficult to adopt. Cultural relativism requires both knowledge and understanding of cultures, which involves extensive effort and study.

However, the problem is alleviated slightly within field of anthropology. Unlike the general public, anthropologists have the means to gain a deep understanding of cultures through their studies. Therefore, cultural relativism is more easily practiced. Returning to the ancient Egyptians, a cultural relativist would examine Egypt not in terms of the technology understood by one's own culture, but only in terms of the Egyptian culture itself. Thus, one would accept that the Egyptians must have built the pyramids. The focus, then, becomes how they built them.

standard:
a basis for judgment

universal:
applicable everywhere in the world

hypothetical:
imaginary; not real

extraterrestrial:
outside of Earth

position:
a set of views

extensive:
complete

alleviate:
to lessen the effects of

Cultural Interpretations

Type 1:
Definition:
Example:

Type 2:
Definition:
Example:

1. According to paragraph 1, which of the following is NOT true of ethnocentrism?
    (A) Anthropologists favor cultural relativity over it.
    (B) It is widespread.
    (C) It can ultimately lead to more culturally relative ideas.
    (D) It applies values globally.

2. Based upon paragraphs 2 and 3, all of the following are true EXCEPT:
    (A) Ethnocentrism is seen in non-anthropologic situations.
    (B) Von Däniken believed aliens were present in ancient Egypt.

    (C) Von Däniken was accused of being ethnocentric.
    (D) There is no evidence to refute who built the pyramids.

3. According to the passage, which of the following is NOT true of cultural relativism?
    (A) It requires an understanding of many cultures.
    (B) It does not believe in universal cultural standards.
    (C) It studies Egypt only in terms of ancient Egyptian culture.
    (D) It is more common than ethnocentrism.

Fill in the blanks to complete the summary.

The passage discusses two ways in which cultures can be understood. The first is ethnocentrism, which is the interpretation of a culture based on the _____ of one's own culture. Ethnocentrism is thought to be a(n) _____ occurrence. Another way to interpret cultures is cultural relativism, which judges cultures according to their own standards. However, this _____ can be difficult to adopt without _____ effort and study of other cultures. Anthropologists help _____ this problem.

----

06 | History

Read the following passage. Then fill in the diagram with the information that you read. `Track 13`

The Globe Theatre

The Globe Theatre, located in London, England, is one of the most famous theaters in the world. During its illustrious history, it was a stage for many of the greatest plays of all time, including those of William Shakespeare. The history of the theater, however, is complex and turbulent. Spanning a period of approximately 400 years, the Globe Theatre underwent three major transformations.

The original Globe was built in 1599 in London's Bankside district and was owned by a number of local actors and playwrights, among them, William Shakespeare. The theater was built using the materials from an earlier theater called, simply, The Theatre. The Globe was constructed as an open-air amphitheater that resembled a twenty-sided polygon. It was three stories high with seats filling its interior perimeter. In the center was the pit, where attendees (called groundlings) would stand and watch the performances. This first structure lasted until 1613, when it was destroyed by fire during a performance of *Henry VIII*.

The Globe Theatre was quickly rebuilt and was completed in 1614. Among the changes to the theater was a new tiled roof to prevent future fire disasters. However, the theater would only remain open until 1642. At the time, the Puritans were the main force in area, closing down theaters and other centers of entertainment. In 1644, the Globe Theatre was demolished to make room for apartment buildings. For the next 350 years, the Globe Theatre would continue to exist only in the minds of its many admirers.

The modern adaptation of the theater was constructed in 1997, and named "Shakespeare's Globe Theatre." The structure of the original Globe Theatre was painstakingly researched and measured to ensure that the new theater would be an accurate replica. Just like the original, the modern theater is an open-air venue. The main difference now is the restrictions laid out by the Health and Safety Department: while three thousand could fit in the original Globe Theatre, only 1,300 are now allowed to be inside at any given time. In addition, electric lights were added to allow for night performances to be held. Unfortunately, the exact location for the Globe Theatre could not be used, so it is now located about 200 meters from its original location.

illustrious:
distinguished

turbulent:
chaotic

span:
to reach or extend over or across something

polygon:
a closed shape with three or more sides

perimeter:
an outline or border

attendee:
someone who participates in or attends an event

admirer:
one who has a favorable impression of something

venue:
the location of an event

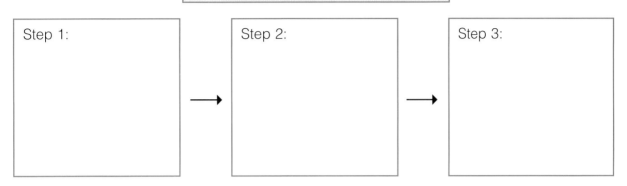

The History of the Globe Theatre

Step 1:

→

Step 2:

→

Step 3:

1. According to paragraph 2, all of the following are true of the first Globe Theatre EXCEPT:

   (A) It was destroyed in 1599.
   (B) It was partially owned by William Shakespeare.
   (C) It was built from the materials of another theater.
   (D) The audience stood in a pit in the center of the theater.

2. According to paragraphs 2 and 3, which of the following is NOT true?

   (A) The theater was rebuilt within a year of its first destruction.
   (B) The Puritans did not allow the theater to remain open.

   (C) The Puritans ordered the theater destroyed in 1642.
   (D) The theater's design was influenced by a disaster.

3. According to paragraph 4, which of the following is NOT true?

   (A) The new Globe is named after William Shakespeare.
   (B) The new theater accurately reproduces the Globe.
   (C) The Globe now has lights for night performances.
   (D) Over 3,000 people can now attend performances.

Fill in the blanks to complete the summary.

According to the passage, London's famous Globe Theatre has a complex and

_____ history _____ about 400 years. Constructed as an open-air

amphitheater, its center was a large pit in which _____ would stand and watch the

performances. After it was destroyed twice, it existed only in the minds of its _____

for 350 years. Finally in 1997, the Globe Theatre was again rebuilt. It is an open-air

_____, just like the original.

Chapter 3 Inference Questions

Necessary Skills

- Perceiving ideas that are suggested but not directly stated within a passage
- Drawing conclusions based on information given within a statement or section of a passage
- Determining logical implications of the author's words

Example Questions

- Which of the following can be inferred about _____?
- The author of the passage implies that _____
- Which of the following can be inferred from paragraph X about _____?
- Based on information in paragraphs X and Y, what can be inferred about _____?
- It is suggested in paragraph X that _____

Strategies

- Ensure that your answer does not contradict the main idea of the passage.
- Do not choose an answer because it seems important or true. The correct answer must be inferable from the passage.
- Check that you can defend your answer choice by referring to explicitly stated information in the passage that points to the inference you have chosen.

01 Literature

Read the following passage. Then fill in the diagram with the information that you read. `Track 14`

Unreliable Narrators

An unreliable narrator is any narrator that cannot be trusted to convey a story accurately. This device is used in literature to force readers to question the narrator's truthfulness. In addition, many authors use unreliable narrators to add a sense of realism to a character.

The use of the unreliable narrator in order to affect the reader's trust in the tale being told is well illustrated in "The Cask of Amontillado" by Edgar Allen Poe. The narrator, Montresor, tells the story of how he was wronged. Already, his view is tainted with prejudice as he expresses his desire to take revenge. As the story progresses, the reader begins to distrust his account further as the symptoms of his psychological illness are revealed. Thus, the reader must contemplate the character's tale and make his or her own decisions about what to believe.

An unreliable narrator can also give a character an added sense of realism. Many authors realize that people do not always tell the truth. They may misinterpret situations, and writers structure their characters accordingly. In the case of Poe's Montresor, had Poe depicted him as a truthful, reliable narrator despite his mental instability, the representation would not have been realistic. However, Poe chose to tell the story as Montresor would have told it, thereby giving the reader a more comprehensive understanding of his character.

device:
a tool

realism:
the quality of being true to reality

taint:
to contaminate

contemplate:
to think about

comprehensive:
complete

Unreliable Narrators

Definition:

Role 1:

Role 2:

1. What can be inferred about unreliable narrators?

   (A) Most readers believe their lies.
   (B) They were first created by Poe.
   (C) They are very clever characters.
   (D) They may be male or female.

2. Which of the following can be inferred about Montresor?

   (A) His illness is not known at the beginning of the story.
   (B) It is difficult for readers to interpret his narration.
   (C) Poe was not aware that he was an unreliable narrator.
   (D) He is the hero of the story.

3. What does the author of the passage imply about realism?

   (A) Realism cannot be present in normal characters.
   (B) Readers find complex characters more realistic.
   (C) Montresor's mental illness is unrealistic.
   (D) Characters that lie are often more realistic.

Fill in the blanks to complete the summary.

According to the passage, an unreliable narrator is a literary _____ that is used to challenge the reader's trust. Unreliable narrators are also used by authors to add a sense of _____ to a character. The example used is "The Cask of Amontillado" by Edgar Allen Poe. The unreliable narrator in this case is Montresor, whose view is _____ with prejudice and a desire for revenge. Readers must _____ whether or not to believe the unreliable narrator, thereby gaining a more _____ understanding of the character.

---

02 Business

Read the following passage. Then fill in the diagram with the information that you read. `Track 15`

Entrepreneurs

An entrepreneur is a person who takes the risk of starting and managing a business venture in order to make a profit. Many new businesses fail—some studies estimate the failure rate as high as seventy-five percent. Nonetheless, experts believe that two things contribute to success in entrepreneurialism: innovation and a willingness to take calculated risks.

Innovation is necessary in new businesses. The goal is to meet an unsatisfied demand. This requires creativity, the driving force behind innovation. Innovation is particularly important for entrepreneurs attempting to break into e-commerce, or businesses that buy and sell over the Internet. The Internet can provide consumers with both convenience and lower prices. Jeff Bezos, the founder of Amazon.com, realized that many consumers wanted books at discounted prices. They did not care where or how they bought them, and in fact, many preferred to have the books delivered to their homes. Bezos, certain that online demand could be strong, started the first major online bookstore, which is now highly successful.

The ability to take calculated risks is another key component of a new business. Unlike working in an already established business or organization, an entrepreneur enters a territory in which success is not guaranteed. Thus, the entrepreneur is taking a unique financial and personal risk. Debbi Fields, the owner of Mrs. Fields, a highly successful chain of cookie stores, was told to stay out of the business. People said that no one would buy her cookies, since cookies are available in supermarkets everywhere. Nonetheless, she felt there was a strong demand for fresh, hot cookies. At last, she convinced a bank to finance her homemade cookie business concept in the late 1970s. Her risk paid off—her company is worth over 450 million dollars today.

venture:
a risky business investment

innovation:
a new or unique product or method

calculated risk:
a risk taken only after carefully considering the results

founder:
a person who starts a business, organization, or nation

component:
a part

established:
existing

territory:
an area or field

finance:
to supply with money

Successful Entrepreneurship	
Requirement 1:	Example:
Requirement 2:	Example:

1. Which of the following can be inferred from paragraph 1 about business?
   (A) New businesses require a significant financial investment.
   (B) Entrepreneurs cannot compete with larger businesses.
   (C) Businesses that are not innovative never succeed.
   (D) Only a quarter of all new businesses are successful.

2. What does the author suggest about the founder of Amazon.com?
   (A) He had great difficulty in opening up this business.
   (B) He can interpret what the consumer really wants.
   (C) He worked in a bookstore before starting his business.
   (D) He hopes to move into other areas of e-commerce.

3. According to paragraph 3, what can be inferred about the cookie company?
   (A) It is the most successful cookie company in history.
   (B) It was originally not popular with customers.
   (C) Its success is due mainly to bank financing.
   (D) It would not have succeeded without risk-taking.

Fill in the blanks to complete the summary.

According to the passage, entrepreneurialism is the launching of a business _____ in order to make money. Two factors that can bring about success in new business are _____ and risk-taking. Innovation is crucial in fulfilling a unique public demand. Risk-taking is another necessary _____ of a new business because many entrepreneurs are competing in a new or difficult _____. For example, the owner of a successful cookie chain had to convince a bank to _____ her business concept in order to become successful.

03 | Biology

Read the following passage. Then fill in the diagram with the information that you read. `Track 16`

Carl Linnaeus

Carl Linnaeus (1707-1778) was a Swedish botanist, explorer, and physician. He is best known for establishing a system of species classification and naming called the *Systema Naturae*. The creation of this system was a lifelong process for Linnaeus, and the result of his work is a system of classification that is still in use today.

Linnaeus's love of plants began during his childhood. Linnaeus's father introduced Carl to botany at a very young age, and his interest grew quickly. By the age of eight, Linnaeus had acquired the nickname "the little botanist." Linnaeus later enrolled at a university to study medicine. However, much of his time at university was spent working with plants, as plants were common in medicinal treatments. During this time, he began to record plant species and attempt to separate them into categories.

The next stage of Linnaeus's career began after his graduation. Despite financial hardship, Linnaeus embarked upon two botanical expeditions in 1731 and 1734 in order to discover more plants that could be added to his growing list. Then, in 1735, Linnaeus's friend and fellow botanist Jan Fredrik Gronovius published the first version of *Systema Naturae*. However, realizing that his classifications were far from complete, he set out on many more expeditions.

His expeditions ceased, however, when Linnaeus became a professor at the University of Uppsala in 1741. He soon became famous in Sweden for his botanical work. During his tenure as a professor at Uppsala, many of his students set out on similar expeditions around the world to gather plant species. In addition, Linnaeus had gained some renown worldwide, and many people sent him plant specimens from their native countries. His *Systema Naturae* grew considerably during this time; what had begun as a small pamphlet had grown into an extensive, multivolume work. Following Linnaeus's death in 1778, scientists continued his work.

botanist:
one who studies plants

hardship:
a difficult condition

expedition:
a journey

tenure:
a period of holding a title or office

renown:
fame

specimen:
a sample of a material

considerably:
to a great extent

pamphlet:
a small published work of information

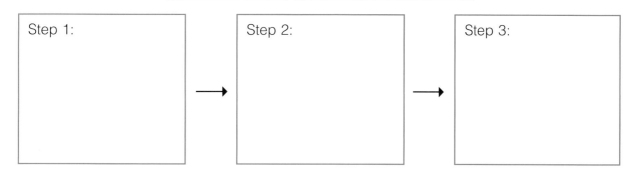

The Botanical Career of Carl Linnaeus

Step 1:

→

Step 2:

→

Step 3:

1. Which of the following can be inferred from paragraph 2 about Linnaeus?

   (A) He was not a good student.
   (B) His medicinal plants are no longer used today.
   (C) He was not actually interested in studying medicine.
   (D) His father influenced his career.

2. Which of the following can be inferred from paragraph 3?

   (A) *Systema Naturae* originally contained many errors.
   (B) Linnaeus graduated from university before 1731.
   (C) Linnaeus traveled with Gronovius.
   (D) A friend financed Linnaeus's expeditions.

3. Which of the following can be inferred from paragraph 4?

   (A) Linnaeus took his students on botanical expeditions.
   (B) Linnaeus's discoveries were not famous outside of Sweden.
   (C) Linnaeus traveled to new countries during his professorship.
   (D) More species were added to *Systema Naturae* after Linnaeus's death.

Fill in the blanks to complete the summary.

According to the passage, Carl Linnaeus was a(n) _____ who dedicated his life to creating a classification system of plants. The process began with a love of plants as a child. Linnaeus set out on many _____ to find new plants. As a professor, he gained worldwide _____ and collected many plant _____ from around the world. His *Systema Naturae* grew _____ into a multivolume work that was preserved by other scientists after his death.

04 | Psychology

Read the following passage. Then fill in the diagram with the information that you read. `Track 17`

Fuzzy Trace Theory

Psychologists have theorized that schemas and other processing methods play a role in the phenomenon of generating false memories. A theory presented by Reyna and Brainerd is called the fuzzy trace theory. Essentially, the theory states that during any event, the brain makes traces of important information from that event. These traces can be separated into two distinct categories: gist traces and verbatim traces. Each category of traces has a role in the creation of false memories.

Fuzzy trace theory defines a gist trace as a mental image that provides a general sense of the entirety of an event. A person participating in any event, then, would likely remember the most important parts of it. However, a gist trace does not provide specific details from the event. Minute details such as names, words, or faces may not be included in the person's memory of the event. Therefore, the mind may create a false memory to fill the gap created by the absence of one or more of those details. For example, after one's participation in a soccer game, one may remember that the outcome was a victory. However, the player may forget a specific detail, such as the period in which a teammate scored a goal. The player's mind may then create a false memory: he or she may remember that the teammate scored in the second half when, in fact, the goal was scored in the first half.

Conversely, a verbatim trace focuses on a specific detail. These traces are often item-based. The focus is on a particular item or perhaps a specific moment from an event. A focus on details can cause false memories of the overall structure of an event because the memory creates only verbatim traces that omit the essence of the events. Many medical patients claim to have forgotten entire events, though in their memory they can recall specific details. For example, a medical patient may say that he or she has forgotten what happened over a number of hours, though he or she remembers specific details, such as street signs, faces, and so on. In the absence of the gist of the event, a false memory may be created to fill in the memory gap. The memory, then, will include the correct details inserted into an incorrect series of events.

schema:
a pattern used to aid in understanding

phenomenon:
an occurrence or circumstance

gist:
the essence or main part of something

verbatim:
using identical words

entirety:
the state of being complete

gap:
an opening or break

outcome:
a result

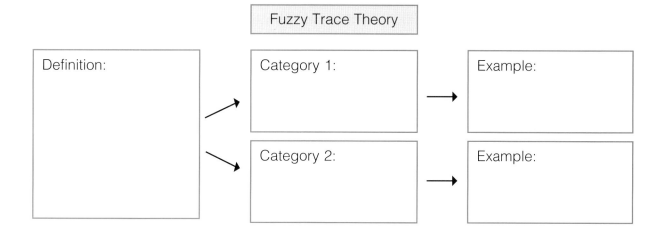

1. Which of the following can be inferred from paragraph 1?
   (A) Multiple theories exist to explain false memories.
   (B) Psychologists often deal with strange phenomenon.
   (C) Reyna and Brainerd created two different theories.
   (D) Gist traces are more common than verbatim traces.

2. According to paragraph 2, what does the author suggest about gist traces?
   (A) They occur often during sports matches.
   (B) They fill in gaps with false memories.
   (C) They blur the smaller details of an event.
   (D) They include both specific and general details.

3. Which of the following does the author imply in paragraph 3?
   (A) Gist and verbatim traces are not related.
   (B) Verbatim traces do not create false memories.
   (C) Most medical patients use verbatim traces.
   (D) Verbatim traces are a common medical issue.

Fill in the blanks to complete the summary.

According to the passage, the _____ of generating false memories can be explained by the fuzzy trace theory. This theory states that after an experience, the brain makes traces of information. A(n) _____ trace is a remembrance of the event in a general sense. Because the brain remembers a general sense of the _____ of an event rather than specific details, false memories may be created to fill in the _____. A(n) _____ trace is a recollection of events based on specific details or moments, rather than the experience as a whole.

05 Astronomy

Read the following passage. Then fill in the diagram with the information that you read. `Track 18`

The Origin of Lunar Craters

The moon is the Earth's only natural satellite, orbiting around the Earth from an average distance of 238,000 miles. According to the giant impact theory, another forming planet collided with our planet about 4.5 billion years ago, causing large pieces of the Earth to leave the atmosphere and go into orbit around the Earth. Later, these pieces underwent a process in which they combined, melted, cooled, and subsequently formed the moon. After its formation, numerous craters, which are characteristic of the jagged terrain of the moon, began to form. The vast majority of lunar craters were created by impacts, although volcanic activity may also have caused craters to appear.

An impact crater is formed when a meteorite hits the surface. Some planets and moons contain atmospheres that are able to burn up meteorites due to the heat produced from air resistance as they enter the atmosphere. The moon does not have an atmosphere. Therefore, it has no protective barrier to burn meteorites up before they reach the surface. Instead, meteorites forcefully explode upon impact, ejecting surface material at great velocity. The force of the impact causes smaller pieces to shoot out from the impact site. The ejected surface material falls back down and showers the moon's surface, creating a raised ring around the crater. Larger craters are created by the impact of asteroids, which are much larger than meteorites.

Volcanic craters form when hot magma, which is molten rock beneath the surface, rises upward, breaking open the surface layers. Since the moon has no moving plates, there are no upper mantle layers as there are on the Earth. Upper mantle layers generally remain intact, so eruptions from below the surface are less likely to occur. Because of the lack of mantle layers on the moon, the magma breaks right through the surface. Through these cracks, hot gases escape as the magma cools and recedes. Through this process, a cavity beneath the surface is formed, and it quivers from the lack of support. As magma has low viscosity, it does not have enough matter to fully form a plateau above the surface. As the surface collapses, the magma falls with it, forming a crater. Volcanic craters differ from impact craters in appearance with their irregular shapes and presence of volcanic matter.

terrain:
an area of land

vast:
very large

barrier:
a structure that prevents passage

eject:
to push out forcefully

velocity:
speed

molten:
melted

viscosity:
the property of a fluid that causes it to resist flowing

plateau:
a raised area of land that is flat at the top

| Lunar Craters |

| Type 1: | | Explanation: |

| Type 2: | | Explanation: |

1. What can be inferred from paragraph 1 about the moon?
   (A) It used to orbit much closer to the Earth.
   (B) Its atmosphere disappeared after formation.
   (C) Its interior was very hot at one time.
   (D) Volcanoes may form there sometime in the future.

2. Which of the following can be inferred based on the information in paragraph 2?
   (A) The process of crater creation continues even now.
   (B) Meteorite craters are more common than asteroid craters.

   (C) Meteorite impacts affect the atmosphere of the moon.
   (D) Asteroid impacts do not create raised rings.

3. According to paragraph 3, what can be inferred about volcanic craters?
   (A) They probably create strong earthquakes on the moon's surface.
   (B) Their formation relates to the lack of a lunar atmosphere.
   (C) They can be identified by their age.
   (D) They would be more common on Earth if it lacked a mantle.

Fill in the blanks to complete the summary.

The moon has accumulated a number of craters that form its jagged _____.
The _____ majority of lunar craters are caused by the impact of meteorites and
asteroids. Because the moon has no atmosphere, there is no protective _____ to
burn up meteorites before they hit the moon's surface. Therefore, when meteorites explode
upon impact, surface material is _____ with great force. Another way lunar craters
are formed is when _____ rock rises through the moon's surface, breaking it. A
cavity forms beneath the surface, which eventually collapses to form a crater.

----

06 Zoology

Read the following passage. Then fill in the diagram with the information that you read. `Track 19`

Similarities Between Dogs and Wolves

The wolf is the ancestor of all domestic dogs. Evidence from Israel indicates that humans domesticated wolves over 12,000 years ago. Today, dogs and wolves exist as a separate species, even though their genetic makeup is nearly identical. While most dogs bear little physical resemblance to the wolf, dogs retain many behavioral characteristics common to wolves. Modern dogs display similarities to wolves in social structures and in their displays of aggression.

The structure of the wolf pack can be seen amongst families of dogs. Both species evolved as a group of social hunters who had to work as a team to kill large animals. Wolves have hierarchical pack structures, in which one wolf acts as the leader and other wolves are expected to be submissive to the leader. Within families, the mother and father are the alpha wolves, and pups are expected to obey. Wolves form hierarchies not only within their families, but also within their packs. Should they try to assert power, those at the bottom of the scale of dominance risk being ostracized by pack leaders. The hierarchy and teamwork of wolves can also be seen amongst dogs, such as the sled-pulling Siberian huskies. The sled-driver acts as the alpha male or female, giving instructions to the pack. The entire group forms a pack hierarchy, which is vital to the success of the sled.

Both dogs and wolves are highly territorial and will show aggressive behavior in order to assert power. Wolves and dogs similarly curl their lips and snarl when attempting to intimidate or threaten. Wolves may fight within their hierarchies, often until one wolf is severely injured. This struggle to show dominance is a common theme in the history of both dogs and wolves. While domestication could tame their wild natures to an extent, dogs have still retained their inherent belligerence and suspicion of strangers, which humans have learned to take advantage of for guarding, hunting, and sports. While modern dogs do not howl in the same way that wolves do, their vocal defense of territory shows many similarities to how wolves defend their homes. Just as a wolf bares its teeth and displays aggression when threatened, a dog behaves similarly if it encounters an unfamiliar or threatening animal.

resemblance:
the state of being similar to something

alpha wolf:
the wolf considered the leader of the pack

ostracize:
to exclude from a group

territorial:
defensive of a particular area

inherent:
existing as a necessary attribute

belligerence:
the state of treating with disdain or aggression

bare:
to reveal or show

Wolves and Dogs

Theory:

Support 1:

Support 2:

1. According to paragraph 2, what can be inferred about wolves?

    (A) Both males and females can be pack leaders.
    (B) Wolf cubs often try to become the alpha male.
    (C) Packs do not exhibit hierarchical relationships.
    (D) The oldest wolf in a pack becomes the alpha wolf.

2. What can be inferred from paragraph 2?

    (A) Dogs do not naturally feel a sense of teamwork.
    (B) A sled driver is considered the most powerful animal.

    (C) Humans are harmful to both wolves and sled dogs.
    (D) Wolf hierarchy is not present in dogs.

3. According to paragraph 3, what does the author imply about wolves?

    (A) They howl when they are happy.
    (B) They enjoy fighting.
    (C) They are better guards than dogs.
    (D) They are suspicious of strangers.

Fill in the blanks to complete the summary.

According to the passage, while dogs and wolves bear little physical _____
to each other, they demonstrate common traits. For example, their social structures consist
of hierarchies within packs or families. They are also both highly _____ and
become aggressive to assert dominance and ownership. Wolves and many dogs have a(n)
_____ _____ toward strangers. They react to a threat by
_____ their teeth and displaying other aggressive behavior.

Chapter 4

Rhetorical Purpose Questions

Necessary Skills

- Determining why the author has presented a piece of information in a certain place or way within a passage
- Understanding the role of a certain statement in a passage
- Inferring the author's intention in mentioning certain information
- Relating specific information to the main ideas of a passage in order to understand the purpose of the information

Example Questions

- The author discusses _____ in paragraph X in order to
- Why does the author mention _____?
- The author uses _____ as an example of

Strategies

- Learn and understand the meaning of certain words and phrases often used to describe rhetorical purposes: *definition, example, function, to illustrate, to explain, to contrast, to refute, to note, to criticize.*
- Focus on logical links between sentences and paragraphs in a passage.

01 Literature

Read the following passage. Then fill in the diagram with the information that you read. `Track 20`

Theme

In literature, the theme is the general idea that is expressed throughout the piece. The theme of a poem is rarely obvious, and it may be difficult to interpret the theme right away. However, by paying attention to certain elements in the poem, it is easier to discern what the theme is.

The first element that can indicate theme is the title of the poem, as it contains the first words the reader encounters. Therefore, it can supply information about what the author wishes to express. Consider the poem "A Boat beneath a Sunny Sky," by Lewis Carroll. This title suggests a peaceful afternoon and happy times. From simply analyzing the title, the reader can assume that the theme will involve a joyful, tranquil experience.

Sometimes, however, the title is not enough to unearth the theme of a poem. Another way to find the theme of a piece of literature is by analyzing repeated words or images. In "A Boat beneath a Sunny Sky," Carroll repeatedly mentions dreams: dreams that linger over the evening and dreams that help the days go by. In the final line, Carroll writes: "Life, what is it but a dream?" By analyzing the repeated words, the reader can conclude that the theme of the poem is to appreciate the dream-like qualities of life.

interpret:
to find the meaning of something

discern:
to tell apart or distinguish

indicate:
to show clearly

tranquil:
calm

unearth:
to discover by searching thoroughly

linger:
to take a long time doing something

conclude:
to decide upon

Identifying Theme

Step 1:	→	Step 2:

1. Why does the author discuss the title of a poem?
   (A) To demonstrate how to interpret a poem's title
   (B) To explain how to find the theme of the piece
   (C) To provide an example of poems with long titles
   (D) To argue that the theme is rarely revealed in the title

2. Why does the author mention a peaceful afternoon and happy times?
   (A) To provide a theory about why the author changed the title
   (B) To refute a previous point about the creation of titles
   (C) To show what the title suggests about the poem's theme
   (D) To note the masterfulness of the poet in describing the scene

3. The author uses dreams as an example of
   (A) the ways that titles can be misleading
   (B) how repeated words can reveal a poem's theme
   (C) the main theme of "A Boat beneath a Sunny Sky"
   (D) common themes in children's literature

Fill in the blanks to complete the summary.

The focus of the passage is on literary themes and how to _____ themes in poetry. A theme is the general idea that is expressed in a poem. The author describes two ways of _____ themes in poetry. First, the reader can analyze a title, which often _____ what the poem may be about. For example, Lewis Carroll's "A Boat beneath a Sunny Sky" suggests that the poem is about something joyful and _____. Next, the reader should look for repeated words or images, as they often help the reader _____ the theme of the poem.

---

02 Meteorology

Read the following passage. Then fill in the diagram with the information that you read. `Track 21`

Aurora Borealis

Meteorologists study weather patterns on the Earth. Many of the spectacular phenomena that can be witnessed from the Earth do not originate on our planet. Rather, some are caused by powerful storms in space, like Aurora Borealis. Aurora Borealis is an extra-planetary storm that causes impressive lights to appear in the northern sky. These lights are only visible from areas in the northern half of the Earth.

Aurora Borealis begins when a cloud of particles is discharged from the sun. The cloud, called plasma, travels through space very quickly. The particles in the plasma are negatively charged, meaning that they contain electrons. When the plasma approaches the Earth, it comes into contact with atmospheric gases.

The gases in the atmosphere help protect the Earth from the sun's rays, but when the charged particles collide with the gases, electricity is transmitted. This is because the atmospheric gases are good conductors of electricity. The collision of plasma and atmospheric gases causes the atoms to become excited, and they build up energy.

When the stored energy is released, the atoms emit light. The spectrum of colors changes continuously during the storm. A green glow can persist for hours, especially if there are no new collisions between atmospheric gases and plasma. From higher altitudes, a red glow is often witnessed.

spectacular:
exciting to look at

originate:
to come from

extra-planetary:
referring to something that occurs outside of a planet

impressive:
causing admiration

discharge:
to release or let out

collide:
to crash into

spectrum:
a range of colors

How Aurora Borealis Is Formed

Step 1:

Description:

Step 2:

Description:

Step 3:

Description:

1. The author describes Aurora Borealis as an extra-planetary storm in order to
   (A) emphasize that it is a massive and powerful storm
   (B) show that Aurora Borealis affects the weather on Earth
   (C) contrast Aurora Borealis with other storms in outer space
   (D) note meteorological phenomena outside of the Earth

2. Why does the author mention plasma?
   (A) To give the proper scientific term
   (B) To explain the importance of plasma
   (C) To provide an example of solar discharge
   (D) To contend the role of plasma is minimal

3. The author discusses altitude in paragraph 4 in order to
   (A) explain the effect of the Earth's atmosphere on the plasma
   (B) illustrate the height to which the Aurora Borealis can be seen
   (C) show that without electrons, the storms would lack their colors
   (D) describe a factor that affects the colors of Aurora Borealis

Fill in the blanks to complete the summary.

According to the passage, many of the _____ weather phenomena seen from Earth are caused by powerful storms in space. For example, Aurora Borealis is an extra-planetary storm that results in the appearance of _____ lights in the northern sky. Aurora Borealis is caused when particles are _____ from the sun. Then, the particles _____ with gases in the Earth's atmosphere. In the process, an electric charge is transferred to the gases. The collision causes energy to build up. When the energy is released, the gases emit lights with a continuously changing _____ of colors.

---

03 Environmental Science

Read the following passage. Then fill in the diagram with the information that you read. `Track 22`

The Electric Car

The invention of automobiles in the 19th century had a profound effect on modern transportation. Further advancements in the automotive industry have led to the development of the electric car. Electric cars are able to function on electric power instead of gasoline fuel. The merits of the electric car have been debated since its invention. However, due to growing concerns about the environmental costs and economic sustainability of gasoline fuel, the electric car is being hailed as the best alternative available to consumers today.

Most modern vehicles employ an internal combustion engine. In order to run, the fuel reacts with air in a small space and produces energy. When internal combustion engines first became popular, there was little concern for the negative effects they might have on the environment. Scientists have since learned that they produce gases and fumes that contribute to air pollution. There are also increasing concerns about the role of carbon dioxide emissions on global warming. Many feel that automobiles are a major cause of the problem. Electric cars are a good alternative to internal combustion engines. They do not directly produce any harmful emissions. According to a scientific study, electric cars reduce carbon dioxide emissions by as much as one hundred percent, especially if solar or wind power is the source of electrical energy.

In addition, electrical cars are also better for the economy. They reduce dependence on petroleum, a non-renewable energy source that powers most internal combustion engines. As the world's supplies of petroleum are depleted, it becomes increasingly expensive for consumers. The fluctuating price of petroleum can cause already unstable economies to collapse. In contrast, electric cars rely less on non-renewable energy sources. The increased use of electric cars lessens the importance of petroleum in the world economy. Moreover, since it is less expensive to produce electricity than gasoline, the cost of operating an electric car is more affordable for consumers.

profound:
in an extreme way

merit:
an advantage

sustainability:
the ability to be maintained

fume:
a harmful vapor or gas

emission:
a substance released into the air

fluctuate:
to change constantly

collapse:
to fail

Electric Cars

Theory:	Support 1:
	Support 2:
	Support 3:

1. Why does the author mention internal combustion engines?
   (A) To explain how electric cars function
   (B) To criticize the amount of fuel used
   (C) To describe the most common type of engine
   (D) To note an advantage of non-electric cars

2. The author discusses carbon dioxide emissions in order to
   (A) argue that electric cars are better for the environment
   (B) note that they can positively impact the ozone layer

   (C) assert that electric cars do not help lower emissions
   (D) define how environmental standards are tested

3. The author uses solar or wind power as an example of
   (A) energy used by internal combustion engines
   (B) a kind of renewable energy used to run electric cars
   (C) a way to make cars run more efficiently
   (D) a type of non-renewable energy for cars

Fill in the blanks to complete the summary.

   The invention of the automobile has had a(n) _____ effect on modern transportation. The passage describes the _____ of the electric car and its benefits to the environment and the economy. Gasoline engines produce gases and _____ that contribute to global warming. Electric cars, meanwhile, can reduce _____ by one hundred percent. Electric cars are also better because they reduce reliance on petroleum. Decreased dependence reduces the impact of _____ petroleum prices on the economy.

---

04 | Biology

Read the following passage. Then fill in the diagram with the information that you read. `Track 23`

Altruism and Evolution

Altruism is selfless behavior that aims to benefit others. It has been examined by philosophers, sociologists, and even biologists. For some biologists, altruistic behavior is strange because it seems to defy Darwin's theory of natural selection. In Darwin's theory, a species is able to continue to survive based on how well adapted it is to the environment. Organisms that possess features to better help them survive are generally regarded as the strongest of the species. But how does a species benefit from altruism? Kin selection theory proposes that altruism is an evolutionary mechanism that promotes species survival by self-sacrifice.

Kin selection is the idea that an organism will place the reproductive success or survival of its relatives above its own in order to help the species. Altruistic behavior that results in the evolutionary success of related organisms is called kin altruism. The theory was first explored by evolutionary biologist W.D. Hamilton, who first observed the phenomenon occurring in social insects, such as ants. He later prepared a mathematical formula, called Hamilton's Rule, which explained how kin selection benefits the genetic fitness of a species. According to Hamilton's Rule, the value of kin altruism can be analyzed in terms of how it either helps or hurts the entire species.

Kin altruism is best illustrated by the bee, a species believed to exercise kin selection. In a hive, there are different types of bees: worker bees, drones, and the queen. Each type has a function that helps the colony survive. The workers collect food and help maintain the hive, the drones defend the hive from enemies, and the queen gives birth to new bees. These types are thought to have evolved because of kin altruism, which favors the queen for reproduction. The workers forgo their ability to reproduce. Even so, by providing safe conditions for the queen, they are able to guarantee the continued survival of the species.

selfless:
unselfish

defy:
to go against

fitness:
the ability for a species to survive

exercise:
to make use of

colony:
a group of animals of the same species that live together

forgo:
to give up

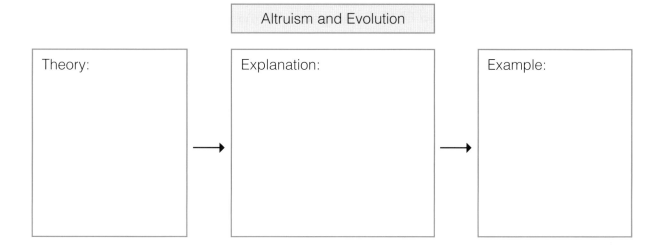

Altruism and Evolution

Theory:

Explanation:

Example:

1. Why does the author mention Darwin?

(A) To introduce the topic of altruism in evolution

(B) To criticize Darwin's theory of natural selection

(C) To question whether altruism and evolution are related

(D) To provide background information about kin selection

2. The author discusses Hamilton's Rule in order to

(A) discredit the scientist's ideas about kin selection

(B) explain how kin altruism can benefit a species

(C) note its importance in understanding altruism

(D) show why some animals favor their relatives

3. The author uses bees as an example of

(A) animals that have not evolved for many years

(B) why altruism is bad for evolutionary success

(C) how animals that practice kin selection get hurt

(D) animals that benefit from kin selection

Fill in the blanks to complete the summary.

The passage discusses altruism in biology. Altruism, or _____ behavior, is considered an evolutionary mechanism that seems to _____ the theory of natural selection. Some scientists believe that by _____ kin selection, some animals promote the genetic _____ of their species by sacrificing themselves. For example, worker bees _____ their ability to reproduce so that they can protect the hive and their queen.

05 Oceanography

Read the following passage. Then fill in the diagram with the information that you read. `Track 24`

Rogue Waves

Rogue waves are extremely large waves that are more than double the average height of most waves. According to mathematical calculations and various personal accounts, rogue waves can reach remarkable heights. They appear unexpectedly in calm waters and can do major damage, even to large ships. Unlike tsunamis, which are practically undetectable in deep water, rogue waves only occur far out at sea. Stories about rogue waves have circulated amongst sailors for centuries, but it was not until recently that scientists confirmed that they actually exist. What they still are not sure of, however, is what causes them.

Some instances of rogue waves have been explained by the interactions of normal wave patterns with ocean currents. Scientists believe that it is possible for waves to reach the heights described when they come into contact with strong ocean currents. The wave heights increase significantly when a normal wave reaches a current head on. In other words, the wave is built up by the power of the current. This explanation was first proposed after scientists observed a high incidence of rogue waves in the ocean surrounding the southern tip of Africa. In fact, since 1990, at least twenty ships have encountered the waves, which reportedly reached up to 190 feet. The waves are thought to be caused by wave interactions with the strong Agulhas Current, which runs southbound along the east coast of the continent.

Ocean currents may be responsible for rogue waves in some parts of the world, but scientists have confirmed their existence even in areas that are not affected by strong currents. In those cases, scientists think that the waves are caused by wave reinforcement. Wave reinforcement is when two or more waves join together to form one massive wave. When the waves are joined, each height is added to the others. For example, if a ten-foot wave comes into contact with a fifteen-foot wave, the resulting wave will be twenty-five feet tall. According to some evidence, it is possible that many waves can join together, which would create rogue waves. Scientists still do not understand which circumstances cause wave reinforcement, but many propose that the reason rogue waves appear suddenly is because they are formed by multiple smaller waves randomly.

account:
a description of an event

undetectable:
unable to be noticed or observed

circulate:
to pass from one person to another

current:
a steady flow of water in one direction

incidence:
the rate at which something happens

massive:
very large

randomly:
occurring without any pattern

| How Rogue Waves Are Formed |

| Theory 1: | → | Support 1: |

| Theory 2: | → | Support 2: |

1. Why does the author mention tsunamis?
   (A) To explain why rogue waves cannot be predicted
   (B) To describe the similar mechanism that causes rogue waves
   (C) To note that rogue waves and tsunamis are unrelated
   (D) To show that rogue waves are comparable to tsunamis

2. The author uses the Agulhas Current as an example of
   (A) how currents become stronger through their contact with ocean waves
   (B) how multiple waves are built up by ocean currents

   (C) a current that flows in the northern region of Africa
   (D) a current that does not affect the wave height in the region

3. The author discusses wave reinforcement in order to
   (A) propose another theory for what causes rogue waves
   (B) suggest that ocean currents cannot be responsible for rogue waves
   (C) demonstrate how rogue waves are created closer to land
   (D) explain how multiple waves are able to interact at sea

Fill in the blanks to complete the summary.

According to many personal _____ and mathematical calculations, rogue waves can reach incredible heights. Stories of rogue waves have _____ for centuries, but scientists still are not sure what causes them. A high _____ of rogue waves off the southern tip of Africa seems to be caused by contact between normal wave patterns and ocean currents. In other areas, rogue waves may be caused by two or more waves joining together to form one _____ wave. However, the exact circumstances in which rogue waves appear are still unknown, and in fact, they may sometimes occur _____.

06 Anthropology

Read the following passage. Then fill in the diagram with the information that you read. `Track 25`

Native American Pottery

Artifacts are ancient objects that have been recovered through archaeological endeavors. Anthropologists study the cultural artifacts left by older societies to gain valuable knowledge about their ways of life. When studying Native American cultures, one common type of artifact is pottery, which can be found all over the continent. By studying the pottery found in a region, anthropologists have been able to learn about ancient techniques, as well as the functions of pottery for Native American peoples. Years of recovering and studying pottery have revealed many differences between the pottery made by people who lived in the southwestern portion of what is now the United States and those who lived in the northeastern region.

Southwestern pottery remains a popular and revered art form. The styles featured in art galleries and museums today have an extensive history. Long before Columbus arrived, southwestern cultures had formed techniques to produce pieces that were beautiful, long-lasting, and functional. Using clay commonly found in the region, Native Americans first created a type of pottery called bisque, which means that it was subjected to extremely hot temperatures to make the material harder, but was not glazed. The pottery was plainly adorned, if at all, suggesting that it held more of a functional purpose than ritualistic.

The pottery of the northeast differed from southwestern pottery in many respects. First, due to the disparate geography, the materials used varied greatly between groups. Rather than just using dried clay, northeastern peoples mixed clay with other materials that were available, such as crushed shells, sand, and plants. Next, the form of northeastern pottery is completely distinctive. Instead of solid pots like those made in the southwest, potters in the northeast formed a rope made of prepared clay. The rope was wound around a circular base, forming coils as the piece was built up. Finally, after the coil pottery was fired, it was further treated with special stones. The natives rubbed the piece with the stones in order to smooth the surface. This final treatment added a polished look to the piece.

recover:
to get something back

revere:
to greatly respect

extensive:
having a great range

subject:
to put something through

glazed:
covered with a layer used to protect the piece

disparate:
different

fire:
to heat objects made of clay to make them harder

```
                          ┌─────────────────────────────┐
                          │   Native American Pottery   │
                          └─────────────────────────────┘

┌──────────────────┐        ┌──────────────────┐        ┌──────────────────┐
│ Type 1:          │   →    │ Materials:       │   →    │ Technique:       │
│                  │        │                  │        │                  │
└──────────────────┘        └──────────────────┘        └──────────────────┘

┌──────────────────┐        ┌──────────────────┐        ┌──────────────────┐
│ Type 2:          │   →    │ Materials:       │   →    │ Technique:       │
│                  │        │                  │        │                  │
└──────────────────┘        └──────────────────┘        └──────────────────┘
```

1. Why does the author discuss southwestern and northeastern artifacts?

   (A) To contrast two types of pottery and their production processes
   (B) To present a key point in the definition of artifacts
   (C) To show the artifacts usually found by scientists
   (D) To explain how different groups influenced each other

2. The author discusses southwestern pot decoration in paragraph 2 in order to

   (A) criticize the artistic talents of the potters
   (B) demonstrate which designs were used
   (C) explain what types of uses they had
   (D) give an example of typical Southwestern pottery

3. The author mentions the stones used in the northeast to describe

   (A) the reason southwestern pots were less smooth
   (B) the process of decorating the pots
   (C) the diverse functions of pots in daily life
   (D) the method used to polish pots

Fill in the blanks to complete the summary.

The passage discusses artifacts _____ in the southwestern and the

northeastern parts of the United States. A popular and _____ art form, the pottery

of southwestern Native Americans has a(n) _____ history. In the beginning, they

created more functional pottery out of clay, _____ it to extremely hot

temperatures. Northeastern pottery featured many different materials due to _____

geography. Native Americans in the northeast also finished pots with stones to add a

polished look.

Vocabulary Review 1

Instructions: Choose the best word or phrase to complete each sentence.

1. After their near defeat on the battlefield, the corporal brought in more troops to _____ the unit's ranks.
   - (A) broach
   - (B) reinforce
   - (C) eject
   - (D) circulate

2. Volunteering to work with the animals at the zoo gave the biology student some good _____ experience.
   - (A) tangible
   - (B) turbulent
   - (C) illustrious
   - (D) hands-on

3. The opening ceremonies featured several hundred performers singing and dancing in _____.
   - (A) string
   - (B) focal
   - (C) unison
   - (D) stratification

4. Although the music was really loud, I could understand the _____ of what he said from his body language.
   - (A) outcome
   - (B) merit
   - (C) chunk
   - (D) gist

5. It was inspiring to see how well the victim _____ after losing her daughter and brother in the crash.
   - (A) coped
   - (B) utilized
   - (C) settled
   - (D) bared

6. A common obstacle in intercultural relationships is overcoming the language _____.
   - (A) terrain
   - (B) compound
   - (C) barrier
   - (D) integration

7. The professor gave a very _____ review before the exam to ensure the students understood the material.
   - (A) undetectable
   - (B) viable
   - (C) embellished
   - (D) comprehensive

8. Young sea turtles, especially those that have just hatched, are particularly _____ to predators like birds, sharks, and monitor lizards.
   - (A) turbulent
   - (B) vulnerable
   - (C) innocent
   - (D) profound

Instructions: Choose the word or phrase closest in meaning to the underlined part of each sentence.

9. Because of the <u>widespread</u> damage done to the area by the earthquake, the government declared a state of emergency.
   - (A) impressive
   - (B) novel
   - (C) extensive
   - (D) prolonged

10. The dentist administered laughing gas to her patient in order to <u>ease</u> his discomfort.

(A) alleviate
(B) integrate
(C) devastate
(D) generate

11. It was time for the accused to give her <u>version</u> of events that occurred on the night of the robbery.

(A) incidence
(B) account
(C) emission
(D) avenue

12. In many western cultures, the white lily is a flower that is <u>representative</u> of purity and sweetness.

(A) verbatim
(B) universal
(C) advantageous
(D) symbolic

13. Although they were twins, the girls bore very little physical <u>likeness</u> to each other.

(A) component
(B) resemblance
(C) specimen
(D) temperament

14. The reporter's weekly <u>review</u> on Hollywood stars and gossip was the network's most popular show.

(A) commentary
(B) expenditure
(C) revenue
(D) impetus

15. When the body is stressed or frightened, adrenaline <u>travels</u> throughout all parts of the body in the blood, keeping energy levels high.

(A) ostracizes
(B) interprets
(C) circulates
(D) originates

Instructions: Write the missing words. Use the words below to fill in the blanks.

discharge	spectacular	indication
	gap	phenomenon

A thunderstorm is a **16.** _____ produced during a cold front and usually lasts an hour or less. The lightning is often considered the most **17.** _____ part of a storm. It is a **18.** _____ of electricity between clouds and the ground. When lightning occurs, it instantly heats the air around it. The hot air expands quickly. After the lightning disappears, the air cools and contracts. This process of expansion and contraction produces sound waves heard as thunder. Counting the **19.** _____ between the lighting and the thunder can give an **20.** _____ of how far away the storm is.

Instructions: Match the words that are similar in meaning.

21. depletion
22. uniform
23. hypothetical
24. prospective
25. transpire

(A) even
(B) potential
(C) reduction
(D) happen
(E) imaginary

Mini Test 1

01 Environmental Science

Read the passage and answer the questions. `Track 26`

Carbon Sinks

When carbon dioxide (CO_2) is released into the air, it acts as a blanket. It keeps heat in the Earth's atmosphere and produces global warming. Global warming causes the Earth's ice to melt, sea levels to rise, and precipitation levels to change. What many do not know is that nature has its own method of counteracting the increased release of carbon into the atmosphere. This takes the form of what climatologists call the carbon sink effect. A carbon sink is anything that acts as a storage area or reservoir for carbon. Oceans and areas with vegetation are natural carbon sinks because they absorb carbon from the air.

The Earth's oceans and areas with growing vegetation are natural carbon sinks. At least one-third of the anthropogenic carbon released on Earth is absorbed by the world's oceans. Young forests with actively growing trees are another area where the carbon sink effect is easily seen. Oceans and forests become carbon sinks through the process of photosynthesis. Photosynthesis occurs when plants take in carbon dioxide for nutrients and, in turn, release oxygen back into the environment. Phytoplankton in the ocean and all the vegetation in the forests are responsible for absorbing carbon dioxide from the air. Carbon can also be absorbed into much of the Earth's soil in the form of organic material, especially in agricultural areas.

Since it is important to reduce the amount of CO_2 in the air, scientists hope to increase nature's ability to form these carbon sinks rather than try to make artificial sinks. Artificial sinks require that carbon first be captured and stored, adding steps and expense to the process. Reforestation is a less expensive way to fight global warming with carbon sinks. The addition of iron oxide or iron sulfate to the world's oceans is another method of increasing carbon absorption. Adding these iron byproducts encourages the growth of plankton. Plankton boosts the amount of carbon absorbed through photosynthesis. As more carbon is absorbed back into nature, less is found in the atmosphere, and global warming attributed to carbon gas is greatly reduced.

▸ **anthropogenic** *produced by humans*

1. Why does the author mention a blanket in paragraph 1?

   (A) To argue that CO_2 is responsible for the carbon sink effect
   (B) To give an explanation of the function of CO_2
   (C) To note that the Earth has too much CO_2
   (D) To illustrate how CO_2 affects Earth's temperature

2. According to paragraph 1, how does CO_2 contribute to global warming?

   (A) It causes the Earth's ice to melt and sea levels to rise.
   (B) It allows more of the sun's heat to enter the atmosphere.
   (C) It reduces precipitation in the air.
   (D) It traps heat in the atmosphere.

3. Which of the following can be inferred from paragraphs 1 and 2?

   (A) CO_2 is the only cause of global warming.
   (B) More carbon sinks would eliminate global warming.
   (C) Carbon sinks cannot form in cities.
   (D) Melting ice contributes to global warming.

4. Which of the following is NOT true about nature's method of carbon sink formation?

   (A) Oceans absorb over one third of the carbon released by human actions.
   (B) The soil in agricultural areas absorbs the majority of the Earth's carbon.
   (C) Forests with young vegetation absorb more carbon than older forests.
   (D) Photosynthesis allows plants to take carbon from the environment.

5. According to paragraph 3, what will reduce the amount of carbon in the air?

   (A) Cutting down on harmful emissions
   (B) Reducing effects of photosynthesis
   (C) Cultivating healthy soil
   (D) Creating more natural carbon sinks

6. All of the following are true about carbon sinks EXCEPT:

   (A) They are storage areas for excess carbon.
   (B) They can reduce CO_2 in the environment.
   (C) They are found mainly in areas with rich soil.
   (D) They can be created through photosynthesis.

7. Which of the following can be inferred about creating artificial carbon sinks?

   (A) Artificial sinks are more beneficial for the environment.
   (B) Natural sinks are preferred over artificial sinks.
   (C) Artificial sinks do not absorb as much carbon.
   (D) Natural sinks absorb more than enough carbon.

8. The author discusses plankton in paragraph 3 in order to

   (A) refute the effectiveness of artificial carbon sinks in the world's oceans
   (B) explain the role of photosynthesis in removing carbon from the atmosphere
   (C) illustrate how adding iron byproducts increases carbon absorption
   (D) criticize the methods scientists are using to try to stop global warming

02 Marketing

Read the passage and answer the questions. `Track 27`

The Influence of Advertising on Pricing

Advertising makes an immense difference in the popularity of a product. Studies have shown that consumers usually pay more for advertised products than non-advertised products. As a result, the marketing and advertising industry is a multibillion-dollar-a-year business. Local commercials can cost as little as several hundred dollars to produce, while national companies have been known to spend hundreds of thousands of dollars on a single commercial. Interestingly, the source for these expensive commercials is the consumers who view the advertisements from the comfort of their living rooms. Companies influence the prices that consumers pay in two ways.

When consumers purchase any product, they are obviously paying for the cost of manufacturing the product. However, they are also paying for the advertising <u>campaign</u> devised to convince consumers to buy the product. The more costly the advertising campaign, the higher the price paid by consumers. Companies are allowed to set these high prices because consumers have shown that they will continue to pay them. For instance, a multinational chain of coffee shops significantly raised its prices a few years ago, due in no small part to an expensive national advertising campaign. While regular customers noticed and were not fond of the hike, one was quoted as saying, "I doubt it will make an impact [on consumers]. It won't change my habit." Indeed, it did not; the company experienced record sales in spite of the fact its prices were higher than its competitors'.

Another way advertising tends to affect product pricing is seen in the arena of perceived value to the consumers. The perceived value is the worth that consumers assign to a product. Studies show that often the advertising for a product determines its value more than the quality or necessity of the product itself. One way a company may take advantage of this perceived value is by running commercials during prime time. These ads are usually much more expensive than others. For example, a national commercial that ran during a popular American show cost close to $745,000 to run for thirty seconds. If people watching the show perceive that the product is more valuable simply because it was advertised during prime time, they are often willing to pay higher prices. So, whether it is seen in the cost of the commercials or the advertiser-assigned value, it is obvious that advertising drives product pricing and directly affects consumers.

▶ **campaign** *a planned and organized series of actions intended to achieve a specific goal*

1. Which of the following can be inferred about pricing and advertising?

   (A) Products that are not advertised cost more than advertised products.
   (B) Customers will pay little for a non-advertised product.
   (C) Companies selling higher-priced products usually advertise more.
   (D) Local companies will not spend money on advertising.

2. How do companies determine the price they charge for a product?

   (A) By determining the overall costs of making the product
   (B) By basing their prices on advertising costs and competitor prices
   (C) By choosing perceived value or manufacturing costs
   (D) By including the cost of advertising in the overall costs

3. Which of the following is true about the effect of higher-priced ad campaigns?

   (A) They increase the price consumers must pay.
   (B) They are a response to consumer demand.
   (C) They result in competitor price matching.
   (D) They have positive effects on customers.

4. The author uses the chain of coffee shops as an example of

   (A) the competitive nature of the advertising industry
   (B) a means by which large businesses deceive consumers
   (C) the acceptance of higher costs by consumers
   (D) a costly advertising campaign that failed

5. According to the passage, which of the following is NOT true about the coffee chain's price increase?

   (A) Many customers stopped buying their coffee there.
   (B) The coffee chain raised prices so they could advertise more.
   (C) Customers acknowledged the change in prices.
   (D) The price increase did not change customers' drinking habits.

6. Which of the following can be inferred from paragraph 3?

   (A) Price is not the only factor affecting buyer decisions.
   (B) Consumers will pay less when they see expensive advertisements.
   (C) The lowest-priced products are usually purchased the most.
   (D) Consumers become angry when prices are raised too high.

7. The author mentions commercials running during prime time in order to

   (A) contrast effective advertising with unsuccessful products
   (B) provide a function of television advertising on a national level
   (C) refute the idea that consumers pay more for products they see on television
   (D) explain how consumers justify paying higher prices for products

8. Which of the following is NOT true about the perceived value of a product?

   (A) It can be higher than the actual value.
   (B) It is influenced by advertising.
   (C) It is partially determined by the consumer.
   (D) It is the same as the true value.

Chapter 5 — Vocabulary Questions

Necessary Skills

- Identifying the meaning of individual words and phrases as they are used in a specific reading passage
- Choosing the correct meaning of a word or phrase in order to understand its relevance within a passage

Example Questions

- The word _____ in the passage is closest in meaning to
- In stating _____, the author means that

Strategies

- Do not choose an answer only because it may be a correct meaning of the word or phrase; choose the meaning that is being used in the passage.
- Try rereading the sentence in which the vocabulary word appears, substituting the answer choices for the word.

01 Linguistics

Read the following passage. Then fill in the diagram with the information that you read. `Track 28`

Vocabulary

Communication between humans is largely based upon language. Learning a new language involves many different processes. One step is to learn and build a vocabulary. Vocabulary is comprised of the different words used by speakers to express themselves. Linguists recognize two different types of vocabulary: passive and active.

The term *passive vocabulary* refers to the set of words that one has learned or is familiar with. Words that comprise a person's passive vocabulary are used infrequently for several reasons. First, their definitions are not always completely known. In other cases, speakers avoid certain words or terms that they do not need to use often in conversation. For most people, their passive vocabulary is much larger than their active vocabulary. This is because passive vocabulary continues to expand throughout a person's lifetime.

Active vocabulary is the set of words that a person can produce, such as when speaking or writing. Many linguists agree that a person's active vocabulary is usually smaller than his or her passive vocabulary. This is because words are only added to the active vocabulary as they are needed. In other words, a person will not add a word to active vocabulary unless he or she needs it to communicate.

linguist:
a scholar who studies language

passive:
not actively in use

avoid:
to stay away from

lifetime:
a period of time that someone lives

produce:
to make something

Vocabulary

Type 1:

Point 1:

Point 2:

Type 2:

Point 1:

Point 2:

1. The word comprised in the passage is closest in meaning to

   (A) learned
   (B) used
   (C) formed
   (D) selected

2. The word infrequently in the passage is closest in meaning to

   (A) not correctly
   (B) not often
   (C) not in a useful way
   (D) not in all situations

3. The word expand in the passage is closest in meaning to

   (A) grow
   (B) understand
   (C) undermine
   (D) overtake

Fill in the blanks to complete the summary.

The passage describes two different types of vocabulary that _____ recognize. Passive vocabulary is the set of words that a person knows but _____ using in speech or writing. A person's _____ vocabulary expands throughout his or her _____. Active vocabulary, on the other hand, is the set of words that a person can actually _____ when speaking or writing.

02 Biology

Read the following passage. Then fill in the diagram with the information that you read. `Track 29`

Origins of Flowering Plants

Angiosperms are the most common type of plant on the planet. All plants classified as angiosperms share a number of traits. The most distinguishing feature of angiosperms, however, is undoubtedly that they produce flowers. At one point, angiosperms cohabited the globe with the dinosaurs. However, unlike dinosaurs, angiosperms not only survived, but thrived.

By studying the fossilized remains of older plants, scientists know that angiosperms evolved to their current form over millions of years. The earliest angiosperm fossil is estimated to be 130 million years old. Other evidence suggests that angiosperm traits existed in plants 250 million years ago. The fossils come from a type of plant called gigantopterids, which resembled ferns. Like angiosperms, the gigantopterid fossils were found to contain a chemical used to protect flowers. This led some scientists to believe that the gigantopterids are the early ancestors of angiosperms—a "missing link" between ancient plants and modern flowers.

The fossil record of angiosperms demonstrates how they diffused across the globe by the mid-Cretaceous epoch, about one hundred million years ago. During this period, the varieties of angiosperms also increased. With the help of bees to spread pollen, angiosperms became the most common type of plant on Earth by the Campanian stage, eighty million years ago.

undoubtedly:
accepted as truth

thrive:
to do well

fossil:
a trace of an animal or plant preserved in stone

estimate:
to guess or approximate

ancestor:
something from which others evolved

diffuse:
to spread

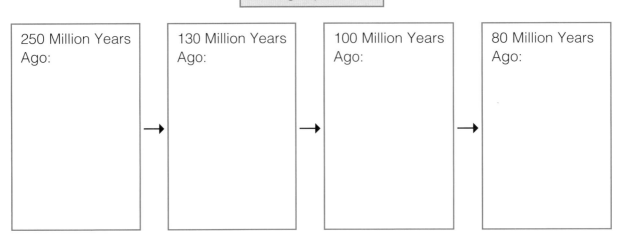

Angiosperms

250 Million Years Ago:	130 Million Years Ago:	100 Million Years Ago:	80 Million Years Ago:

1. The word cohabited in the passage is closest in meaning to

    (A) lived together
    (B) did often
    (C) journeyed
    (D) continued

3. The word pollen in the passage is closest in meaning to

    (A) a common plant disease
    (B) powder from flowers
    (C) early types of flowers
    (D) leaves and stems

2. The word epoch in the passage is closest in meaning to

    (A) variety
    (B) age
    (C) climate
    (D) change

Fill in the blanks to complete the summary.

The passage discusses angiosperms, flowering plants that continued to _____ long after dinosaurs became extinct. The earliest angiosperm _____ is thought to be 130 million years old. It is also _____ that angiosperms began to evolve about 250 million years ago from the gigantopterids. Gigantopterids may be the earliest _____ of angiosperms. Bees helped the plants _____ across the world by spreading the plants' pollen. Angiosperms are now the most common type of plant on Earth.

03 Economics

Read the following passage. Then fill in the diagram with the information that you read. `Track 30`

Inflation

In economics, inflation is the process that leads to increased prices for all goods and services. Generally, inflation is seen as negative because it lowers the value of money. For example, after inflation, one dollar cannot buy as much as it did before inflation. Many factors contribute to inflation, and economists have formulated several theories to explain why it happens. Two popular theories of inflation are demand-pull inflation and cost-push inflation.

The theory of demand-pull inflation is associated with John Maynard Keynes. Keynes was an important 20th-century economist. According to Keynesian economics, demand-pull inflation occurs when the demand for a product, or good, increases. Increased demand means that the product will eventually become scarce. With less of the product available, it costs more for people to purchase it. Thus, consumers effectively bid up the price of the product. Indeed, demand-pull inflation is usually described as a situation in which "too much money is spent chasing too few goods." Economists have isolated several factors that cause demand-pull inflation, such as increases in the supply of currency, in government purchases, or in exports.

Cost-push inflation also originates in Keynesian economics. The theory holds that inflation occurs when the price of production rises significantly. If it costs more to make something, companies must increase the price they charge the consumer in order to remain profitable. This situation is commonly seen when companies increase their employees' wages. If businesses must pay their workers more, they must in turn charge more for the goods or services they produce. Another cause of cost-push inflation is seen when the price of raw materials rises. For instance, if it costs a company more to import metals used in manufacturing, it must pass this increase on to the consumer.

effectively:
in effect

isolate:
to separate something from its other parts

export:
to send goods to another country to sell

production:
the process of making things to be sold

profitable:
able to make money

raw materials:
goods that are not manufactured

import:
to buy products from another country

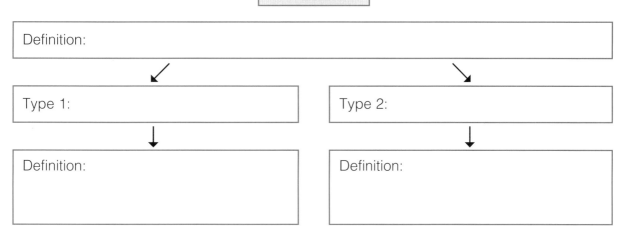

1. The word **formulated** in the passage is closest in meaning to
   (A) researched
   (B) decreased
   (C) conceived
   (D) argued

3. The word **wages** in the passage is closest in meaning to
   (A) price of materials
   (B) money paid to workers
   (C) number of employees
   (D) kind of workplace

2. The word **scarce** in the passage is closest in meaning to
   (A) expensive
   (B) frightening
   (C) popular
   (D) not easy to find

Fill in the blanks to complete the summary.

   The passage discusses two economic theories explaining inflation. The first is demand-pull inflation. This is when supplies are unable to meet consumer demand. By their willingness to pay more for the product, consumers _____ bid up the price. Factors causing demand-pull inflation include an increase in currency or _____. The second type of inflation is cost-push inflation. This occurs when the _____ price of something increases. Companies must charge consumers more in order to keep the businesses _____. Cost-push inflation can also be caused by an increase in the price of _____.

----

04 Photography

Read the following passage. Then fill in the diagram with the information that you read. `Track 31`

Contrast in Photography

In photography, contrast is the degree to which the tones in the picture differ. A high-contrast black-and-white photo, for example, will feature mostly black and white objects with few grey tones. A low-contrast photo, meanwhile, will have very little tonal variation.

A photographer who has paid proper attention to contrast in his or her work will direct a viewer's attention to the most interesting aspect of the photograph. Also, the picture will be more pleasurable overall to look at. There are many different techniques that a photographer can employ to achieve effective contrast in a photo. First, special care must be taken to provide adequate and appropriate lighting. Another way to ensure proper contrast is to regulate the amount of time the film is exposed to light.

When deciding how to light a scene, the photographer must consider how the lighting will affect the contrast on film. Too little lighting and the tonal differences may not be apparent in the photograph. On the other hand, too much lighting may make the subject appear washed out. If relying on natural light, special equipment called filters can be used to improve contrast. Filters are pieces of colored glass that are usually screwed on to the end of the lens. When properly used, the filter can make certain colors appear brighter and others duller.

Aside from determining appropriate lighting for a scene, pleasing contrast can also be achieved. This can be done by paying special attention to the amount of light the film is exposed to when actually taking the picture. In photography, this is called exposure. Exposure can be manipulated by changing either the aperture (the opening in the lens that allows the light to come in) or the shutter speed (the speed at which the window in the camera remains open). Fortunately, choosing the proper exposure time does not take a great deal of technical knowledge of cameras. In fact, by experimenting with the camera, even an amateur can figure out appropriate exposure times for different subjects.

If a photographer is unsure of how long to expose the photo, he or she can also employ a technique called bracketing. Bracketing is when a subject is photographed multiple times using different exposure times. Bracketing allows the photographer to choose which of the exposures will render the best contrast.

tone:
the quality or shade of color

variation:
a small difference in something

direct:
to control something

regulate:
to adjust

apparent:
obvious

filter:
a piece of equipment used to remove certain kinds of light

manipulate:
to control something with hands

render:
to make or cause something

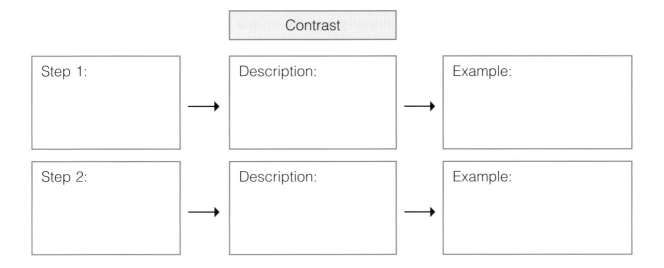

1. The word **degree** in the passage is closest in meaning to
   (A) angle
   (B) variant
   (C) amount
   (D) temperature

2. The word **adequate** in the passage is closest in meaning to
   (A) satisfactory
   (B) bright
   (C) attractive
   (D) careful

3. In stating that too much light will make a subject look **washed out**, the author means that the subject will appear
   (A) clean
   (B) faded
   (C) darker
   (D) in high contrast

Fill in the blanks to complete the summary.

The passage describes ways that photographers can achieve effective contrast in photographs. Proper contrast in a photograph will _____ the viewer's attention to its most interesting aspects. One way is to _____ the amount of time the film is exposed to light. By using lens _____, photographers can accentuate certain colors and reduce others. The other way that photographers control contrast is by exposing the film correctly. Exposure can be _____ by changing the aperture or the shutter speed. A technique called bracketing can allow a photographer to choose an exposure that will _____ the best contrast in a photograph.

---

05 Health

Read the following passage. Then fill in the diagram with the information that you read. `Track 32`

Fatigue

Fatigue is the feeling of extreme weariness or exhaustion. At some point, everyone feels the effects of fatigue, whether it is after a long run or a hard day of studying. However, not many people know about the different types of fatigue. The three main types of fatigue are physical, mental, and in extreme cases, pathological. Knowing the types of fatigue can help to identify the behavior that causes it. Or in some instances, the type of fatigue can also provide clues about more serious health conditions that may be present.

Physical fatigue is a familiar feeling for many people. Some describe physical fatigue as feeling drained. It usually occurs after doing rigorous work, like riding a bike or playing a game of soccer. Medical experts define physical fatigue as a condition that keeps someone from performing at a normal level. Physical fatigue is also called muscle weakness. This is because, in a medical sense, one who feels physical fatigue is actually suffering from a loss of muscle function, albeit a temporary one. Physical fatigue usually becomes obvious after some exertion. When the body is forced to work while fatigued, one may experience a burning sensation in the muscles.

A different type of fatigue is mental fatigue. People who suffer from mental fatigue do not always feel the same effects as those who suffer from physical fatigue. In fact, a person who is mentally fatigued is often afflicted with drowsiness. In other cases, a mentally fatigued person may not feel sleepy, but find it very difficult to concentrate. Mental fatigue can occur because of many different factors. Stress and overwork are common causes. Interestingly, one of the top causes of mental fatigue is boredom. As with physical fatigue, mental fatigue can be harmful if it interferes with daily activities such as driving.

Many people experience either physical or mental fatigue on occasion. For some people, however, fatigue is a constant condition. When fatigue causes discomfort or often interferes with daily activities, it could be pathological. Pathological fatigue may be an indicator of a more serious health problem, such as chronic fatigue syndrome (CFS). CFS is a disorder that causes sufferers to experience constant physical and mental fatigue. A commonly misunderstood disease, CFS is one example of how fatigue can take on pathological proportions.

weariness:
the state of feeling tired or lacking energy

pathological:
relating to or caused by a disease

drained:
lacking energy

temporary:
not lasting a long time

exertion:
the state of using energy; effort

drowsiness:
the state of being sleepy

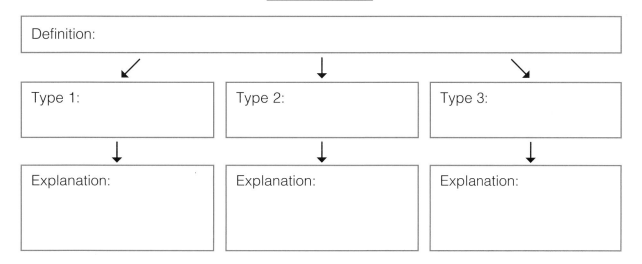

1. The word rigorous in the passage is closest in meaning to

   (A) severe
   (B) demanding
   (C) precise
   (D) forceful

2. The word albeit in the passage is closest in meaning to

   (A) although
   (B) moreover
   (C) yet
   (D) all ready

3. The word interfere in the passage is closest in meaning to

   (A) go into
   (B) get in the way of
   (C) lose influence
   (D) lose concentration

Fill in the blanks to complete the summary.

The passage discusses three types of fatigue, the feeling of extreme _____ or exhaustion. Physical fatigue can be described as feeling _____, and is caused by physical exertion. This type of fatigue is a(n) _____ loss of muscle function, and is usually pronounced after some type of _____. The second type is mental fatigue. It is characterized by feelings of _____ and difficulty concentrating. The third type is pathological fatigue, which may be caused by a disease such as chronic fatigue syndrome.

06 | Anthropology

Read the following passage. Then fill in the diagram with the information that you read. `Track 33`

The Austronesian Language Group

The word "aborigines" may bring to mind the native peoples of Australia. However, the term also refers to the group of people who originally inhabited Taiwan. The often-ignored indigenous people of Taiwan have a very rich culture and history. They also share a variety of interesting creation myths and fascinating traditions. Although perhaps not widely recognized, according to many anthropologists, prehistoric Taiwan was most likely the seat of Austronesian languages and culture.

The Austronesian language group is thought to include the largest number of languages. One-fifth of all languages in the world belong to the Austronesian family. It is also the most geographically dispersed language group in existence. These languages are widely spoken by native peoples in countries located in the Pacific Ocean. Such countries include Malaysia and Indonesia (where Malay is spoken), the Philippines (Tagalog), and New Zealand (Maori). Surprisingly, Malagasy, the language of the natives in Madagascar off the eastern coast of Africa, is also considered an Austronesian language.

It may seem hard to believe that one of the largest language families could have originated on an island as tiny as Taiwan. Yet, anthropologists have recently uncovered more evidence that confirms this hypothesis. The most convincing data stems from the concept of language dispersion in linguistics. The concept holds that the spread of language can be determined by tracing it to the area with the most linguistic diversity. In other words, a region that is found to have many languages is usually the source of related languages in neighboring regions. In Taiwan, this is certainly the case. In fact, nine out of the ten branches of the Austronesian language group are formed by Formosan languages. Formosan refers to languages spoken by the original inhabitants of Taiwan. This means that languages spoken on the island were likely the basis for most Austronesian languages.

Another way of tracing Austronesian languages to Taiwan is by studying migration patterns of ancient speakers. Archaeological evidence suggests that people (presumably those who spoke Austronesian languages) began leaving Taiwan about 6,000 years ago. Also, studies have uncovered a genetic link between people currently living in Austronesian-speaking countries and the indigenous people of Taiwan. This connection is significant in proving that the language, like the people, probably originated in Taiwan.

ignored:
overlooked; disregarded

confirm:
to prove to be true

hypothesis:
a guess that is made by studying the facts

stem:
to come from or originate in

diversity:
a variety of something

migration:
a population movement from one place to another

Origin of Austronesian Languages

Theory:		Support 1:		Explanation:

		Support 2:		Explanation:

1. The word indigenous in the passage is closest in meaning to

(A) original
(B) angry
(C) old
(D) shy

3. The word dispersed in the passage is closest in meaning to

(A) spoken
(B) learned
(C) spread
(D) central

2. In stating that Taiwan was the seat of Austronesian languages and culture, the author means that Taiwan was

(A) a place to stop
(B) the main focus
(C) the base
(D) the last

Fill in the blanks to complete the summary.

The passage proposes that the often-_____ aborigines of Taiwan are the descendants of the original speakers of Austronesian languages. Anthropologists have uncovered evidence that _____ the origins of this language family. The most convincing data _____ from the fact that languages usually originate in areas with the most linguistic _____. Studies reveal that Formosan languages form nine out of the ten branches of Austronesian language. Scientists also can genetically link peoples from countries that speak Austronesian languages to the ancient inhabitants of Taiwan by studying their _____ patterns.

Chapter 6 — Reference Questions

Necessary Skills

- Identifying the relationships between pronouns and their referents in a passage
- Determining to which person, place, or thing a pronoun refers in the context of a passage

Example Questions

- The word _____ in the passage refers to

Strategies

- Ensure that your answer choice matches the same number (singular or plural) and the person (first, second, third) as the pronoun being asked about.
- Try substituting your answer choice for the pronoun in the passage to see if your choice is sensible.
- Since there is often more than one answer choice that may seem correct, read the sentences around the pronoun's sentence carefully to ensure you choose correctly.
- Remember that the grammatical referent for a pronoun may appear in a preceding clause or sentence.

01 History

Read the following passage. Then fill in the diagram with the information that you read. `Track 34`

The United Nations

The United Nations is an international organization. Its primary goal is to maintain peace among the countries of the world. It is comprised of 193 nations and has existed for over fifty years. The United Nations officially convened for the first time in 1945. However, a series of events preceded its formation.

Before the United Nations came into existence, there was another organization with a similar goal called the League of Nations. It was founded in 1919, shortly after World War I. However, the League of Nations was not effective in enforcing its resolutions. This and other limitations left world leaders wanting a different type of international organization.

The main motivation behind the formation of the United Nations was to avoid another devastating war like World War II. The idea for the United Nations came about during wartime conferences in Moscow and Tehran in the latter part of 1943. When the declarations were signed, an agreement was made that an organization like the United Nations would be created in the future. Over the next year, representatives from China, France, the United Kingdom, Russia, and the United States met in order to outline the basic goals of the organization. They were agreed upon, and the charter was finally approved on October 24th, 1945. This marked the official beginning of the United Nations.

primary:
main

convene:
to come together

precede:
to come before

enforce:
to uphold

resolution:
a formal statement of a decision made by an organization or assembly

devastating:
causing a lot of damage

wartime:
occurring during a war

charter:
a formal statement

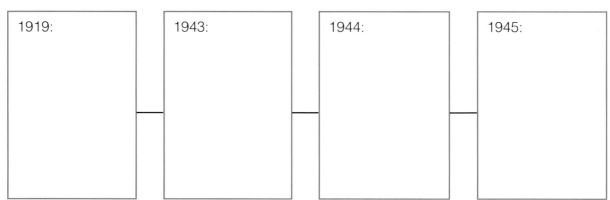

The Formation of the United Nations

| 1919: | 1943: | 1944: | 1945: |

1. The word its in the passage refers to

    (A) sovereign nations
    (B) the League of Nations
    (C) the United Nations
    (D) peace

2. The word It in the passage refers to

    (A) The United Nations
    (B) The League of Nations
    (C) Goal
    (D) Existence

3. The word They in the passage refers to

    (A) Basic goals
    (B) Conferences
    (C) Representatives
    (D) Five countries

Fill in the blanks to complete the summary.

   The passage discusses the history of the United Nations. Another international organization called the League of Nations _____ its formation, but it had been ineffective in _____ its resolutions. World leaders wanted to avoid another _____ world war, so they made an agreement to create a new peacekeeping organization. After a series of _____ conferences with representatives from around the world, the United Nations officially _____ for the first time on Oct 24ᵗʰ, 1945.

----

02 Sociology

Read the following passage. Then fill in the diagram with the information that you read. `Track 35`

Urbanization

Urbanization describes a population shift from rural communities to large cities. More and more, countries are encountering problems with the rapidly growing rate of big cities. This is even more of a problem in areas where the population boom has surpassed the city's ability to meet the needs of its people. This has been the case in the Mexican capital, Mexico City. A metropolis of over twenty million people, its resources have become limited. City administrators have been left to deal with problems such as water shortages and heavy traffic. Luckily, city officials are taking new measures to reduce the problems associated with urbanization.

Having a safe and reliable water supply is important to any city in the world. In Mexico City, water shortages have always been a problem. Although the city is situated above an aquifer, it is not enough to supply the overwhelming number of inhabitants with the water it needs. In order to counter the water shortage, city officials have begun to explore options for obtaining water from other sources, namely states that surround the federal district. Additionally, they have launched a city-wide campaign to raise awareness about water conservation among the city's citizens.

The dense population of Mexico City inevitably creates traffic jams that can last for hours. In order for the city to properly function, its inhabitants need to have a way to get around quickly and easily. Mexico City's response to the traffic problem was to form a partnership with an organization. Their partnership will help city administrators improve public transportation. Among the changes is the replacement of old, unreliable buses used for public transportation. This will increase efficiency by avoiding mechanical failures. Moreover, extra routes will be added in order to serve a greater part of the population. The improvement in public transportation is expected to ease traffic congestion by reducing the number of cars on the road.

rural:
characteristic of the country

surpass:
to do better than

metropolis:
a very large and influential city

shortage:
a lack of something

reliable:
able to be trusted or depended upon

aquifer:
an underground source of water

Urbanization in Mexico City

| Problem 1: | → | Solution: |
| Problem 2: | → | Solution: |

1. The word This in the passage refers to

   (A) Population
   (B) Problem
   (C) Rapid growth
   (D) Rural shift

2. The word it in the passage refers to

   (A) Mexico City
   (B) population
   (C) aquifer
   (D) water shortage

3. The word they in the passage refers to

   (A) city officials
   (B) sources
   (C) inhabitants
   (D) water shortages

Fill in the blanks to complete the summary.

     The passage discusses the problems associated with urbanization. A large population shift from _____ communities to large cities can cause great difficulties, especially in areas where population growth _____ a city's ability to meet the needs of its citizens. For example, in the _____ of Mexico City, issues such as water _____ and heavy traffic are a challenge for city officials. Mexican administrators are now exploring options that will provide people with a safe and _____ water supply and efficient public transportation.

----

03 Astronomy

Read the following passage. Then fill in the diagram with the information that you read. `Track 36`

Binary Star Systems

Binary star systems are pairs of stars that move around the same center of mass in space. To explain further, the center of mass is the point on which the mass of a system is concentrated. By studying binary stars, astrophysicists are able to determine the actual mass of stars in the system. There are several types of binary star systems. Each type is classified according to how it is observed.

A visual binary star is one that can be seen through a telescope. Sometimes binary stars cannot be seen through a telescope because they are too close together and simply appear as one star. However, many modern telescopes with high resolving power can distinguish between binary stars. The brighter of the visual binary is called the primary star, and the dimmer is called the secondary star. By measuring the angles of the stars in relation to each other over time, physicists are able to determine the shape of the binary's orbit.

Spectroscopic binary stars are systems that can only be seen with a spectrometer. The spectrometer is able to measure otherwise unperceivable differences in the type of light the stars emit. By watching for spectral lines, astrophysicists can recognize a system in which the stars are too close together to be seen with a telescope.

An eclipsing binary star can be seen when the orbit of the binary is situated along the line of sight for the viewer. As the stars travel along their orbits, they inevitably eclipse each other. By studying eclipsing binaries, scientists are able to learn about the distance to other galaxies with utmost accuracy. Thus, they can increase the available information concerning the composition of space.

concentrate:
to bring together; to focus

resolving:
relating to the ability to show things in detail

orbit:
a path that objects move around

unperceivable:
not able to be noticed

spectral line:
a dark or bright line that is emitted from a continuous spectrum

inevitably:
in a way that cannot be avoided

composition:
the parts that something is made of

Binary Star Systems

| Classification 1: | Explanation: |

| Classification 2: | Explanation: |

| Classification 3: | Explanation: |

1. The word it in paragraph 1 refers to

(A) mass
(B) type
(C) star
(D) system

3. The word they in paragraph 3 refers to

(A) galaxies
(B) eclipsing binaries
(C) scientists
(D) orbits

2. The word they in paragraph 2 refers to

(A) lenses
(B) telescopes
(C) binary stars
(D) scientists

Fill in the blanks to complete the summary.

Pairs of stars that _____ around the same center of mass in space are called binary star systems. The point that the mass of a system is _____ on is the binary star system's center of mass. Visual binary stars can be seen through a telescope with high _____ power. Spectroscopic binary stars can only be seen with a spectrometer, which measures _____ differences in the light the stars emit. Eclipsing binary stars travel along an orbit in which they eclipse each other. Studying eclipsing binary stars allow scientists to determine the _____ of space.

04 | Biology

Read the following passage. Then fill in the diagram with the information that you read. `Track 37`

Tropisms and Nastic Movements

Compared to the busy lives of humans, it would seem that plants are just stationary companions that beautify gardens and brighten rooms. Surprisingly, plants actually move a great deal. From the interweaving of an ivy plant on a pole to the sunflower that cranes its neck to reach for the sunlight, plants are in constant motion. Although their efforts go mostly unnoticed, most plants depend on daily movement in order to get proper nutrition, repel enemies, or reproduce. Two common types of plant movements are tropisms and nastic movements.

Tropism is when a plant moves in response to a stimulus. Moreover, the stimulus is always directional, meaning that the plant will move to face the direction of the stimulus. The movement caused by tropism indicates that the plant is growing, thus making it an irreversible movement. There are many kinds of tropisms. The different types are typically denoted by a prefix that goes before *tropism*. For example, phototropism is movement that responds to light. A familiar example of phototropism is when a houseplant turns and grows toward the brightest source of light available, usually a window. If the houseplant is moved, one would observe that it changes direction yet again and starts growing toward the light. This mechanism helps plants receive enough light to be able to go through the process of photosynthesis and create food.

In contrast, nastic movements are plant movements that occur in response to environmental stimuli, such as temperature or humidity. Unlike tropic movements, they are not directional. Also, because they do not have to do with plant growth, nastic movements are reversible. Different stimuli are responsible for nastic movements. When referring to a specific type, the same system of adding an appropriate prefix to *nasty* is used. For example, a nastic movement that occurs in response to a touch is called thigmonasty. Thigmonasty is the type of plant movement that is responsible for the rapid shutting motion of the carnivorous Venus flytrap. The plant is equipped with highly sensitized hairs on each leaf. When an insect touches the hair, the leaves snap shut, trapping the insect. Although more dramatic than a phototropic houseplant, thigmonasty is just a mechanism that allows the Venus flytrap to secure the nutrients it needs to survive.

stationary:
stuck in one place; not able to move

interweave:
to combine two or more elements so they cannot be separated

crane:
to stretch in order to look at something

repel:
to force away

stimulus:
something that causes growth or activity

mechanism:
a method or means of doing something

photosynthesis:
a process in plants by which light is converted into chemical energy

Plant Movements

| Type 1: | Characteristic 1: |
| | Characteristic 2: |

| Type 2: | Characteristic 1: |
| | Characteristic 2: |

1. The word *their* in the passage refers to

   (A) sunflowers
   (B) poles
   (C) plants
   (D) movements

2. The word *it* in the passage refers to

   (A) indication
   (B) growth
   (C) plant
   (D) tropism

3. The word *they* in the passage refers to

   (A) nastic movements
   (B) tropic movements
   (C) environmental stimuli
   (D) directions

Fill in the blanks to complete the summary.

While plants may appear to be _____ objects, they do in fact move a great deal. For example, ivy plants can _____ with a pole, and sunflowers _____ their faces toward the sun. One type of plant movement is tropism. Tropisms occur when a plant reacts to a directional _____. For instance, phototropism is when a plant moves in response to a light stimulus. Another type of plant movement is nastic movement. It occurs when a plant reacts to environmental changes. Thigmonasty occurs when the plant moves in response to touch. This movement is a(n) _____ that allows plants such as the Venus flytrap to feed.

----

05 Health Sciences

Read the following passage. Then fill in the diagram with the information that you read. `Track 38`

Sugar

Sugar cane has been cultivated since prehistoric times. Thought to have originated in the Pacific island of New Guinea, sugar has found its way to households all over the world. Despite its value, the sweet substance has many negative effects, according to some scientific reports. It has been proven to cause tooth decay, suppress the immune system, and contribute to obesity. But perhaps the most serious of the consequences that result from eating sugar is the possibility of developing a sugar addiction. Sugar addiction is when a person craves food that contains sugar and has a negative reaction in its absence. Scientists have learned that it is possible for humans to become both psychologically and physically dependent on sugar.

Psychological dependence is when the mind becomes reliant on a certain substance or activity in order to feel good. Psychological addictions usually occur when a person tries to relieve other symptoms, like feelings of loneliness or anxiety. Thus, it is easy to see how one might become psychologically dependent on sugar. Numerous studies and surveys have revealed that people seek sugary foods when they are feeling down or angry. In addition, they often report feeling better after indulging in a sweet snack. This suggests that the uncontrollable cravings, anxiety, and even depression experienced when one cannot have sugar are caused by a psychological addiction to the substance.

The possibility that sugar is physically addictive has been a matter of debate for many years. A physical addiction is when a person's body becomes accustomed to the use of a substance. It is characterized by the appearance of withdrawal symptoms when the person stops using the substance. The idea that sugar could trigger physiological changes similar to a drug has been refuted in the past, but recent studies have provided new insight into the legitimacy of this claim.

Experimenters tested rats by offering them sugar-water solutions as well as regular food. Initially, the rats ate both the food and the sugar equally. Within a month, however, scientists observed that they had stopped eating regular food. Moreover, their sugar consumption had doubled. When the sugar was taken away, researchers noted that the rats showed signs of withdrawal, such as paw tremors and teeth chattering. Although similar studies have not been reproduced in humans, the results suggest that sugar might be physically addictive.

cultivate:
to grow

suppress:
to prevent from operating

crave:
to want something strongly

indulge:
to allow oneself to have something enjoyable

withdrawal:
a period when one discontinues use of a substance on which the body is physically dependent

tremor:
a slight shaking movement

Effects of Sugar

Theory 1:	→	Support:
Theory 2:	→	Support:

1. The word This in the passage refers to

   (A) Sugar dependence
   (B) Report feeling better
   (C) Feeling down
   (D) People seek sugary foods

3. The word they in the passage refers to

   (A) rats
   (B) experimenters
   (C) scientists
   (D) solutions

2. The word It in the passage refers to

   (A) Body
   (B) Substance
   (C) Use
   (D) Physical addiction

Fill in the blanks to complete the summary.

The passage discusses the theory that sugar can be addictive. When a person _____ sugary foods and experiences a negative reaction in its absence, he or she may have a sugar addiction. Although sugar cane has been _____ for thousands of years, too much sugar can cause tooth decay and _____ the immune system. According to surveys, people _____ in sugary foods when they are feeling angry or sad. This suggests that sugar is psychologically addictive. Evidence that it may also be physically addictive was revealed after a study on rats. The rats that were dependent on sugar experienced _____ and other withdrawal symptoms when the sugar was taken away.

---

06 Psychology

Read the following passage. Then fill in the diagram with the information that you read. `Track 39`

The Clever Hans Effect

Body language can say a lot about what a person thinks or desires. For many years, psychologists have studied body language to learn about how people communicate by using their bodies. Paralanguage is an important part of communication, not only among humans but between humans and animals as well. Scientists have discovered that some animals seem to be more receptive to cues from humans. One instance of this is documented in the case of Clever Hans, a horse from Germany who would lend his name to the phenomenon called the Clever Hans Effect.

Early in Hans's life, his owner discovered that Hans had an extraordinary talent. Unlike other horses, Hans was able to perform simple arithmetic, tell time, and even keep track of calendars. Wishing to share Hans's talent with the world, his owner took Hans all over the continent to showcase his wondrous skills. But when German psychologist Oskar Pfungst studied Clever Hans, he discovered that Hans was no more skillful at mathematics than any other horse. Instead, he was particularly adept at interpreting human body language.

Pfungst came to this conclusion after many different trials. First, he took Hans away from an audience to make sure the horse was not receiving signals from people watching him. Then Pfungst had people other than the horse's owner ask Hans questions. In both trials, Hans was able to answer the questions correctly, but the horse performed poorly when he could not see the person asking him questions. He also did not perform well in tests where the person asking the question did not know the answer. These results led Pfungst to a groundbreaking discovery. Without intending to, the people asking questions were giving Hans cues about the correct answers. As the horse tapped out his response to a question, his trainer would change his posture when Hans approached the right number. That was why he could not give the right answer when the trainer did not know it. Furthermore, without being able to see the trainer, Hans could not tell when he should stop tapping his foot.

Pfungst's discovery was important in many respects. It helped scientists thereafter design experiments in which testers could not influence the results through subtle, often involuntary cues. It also brought to light problems that occurred not only with animal test subjects, but human subjects as well.

paralanguage:
communication that does not involve speech or verbal utterances

receptive:
able to listen to ideas

cue:
a signal

document:
to record the details of an event

showcase:
to display something

adept:
having natural ability to do something well

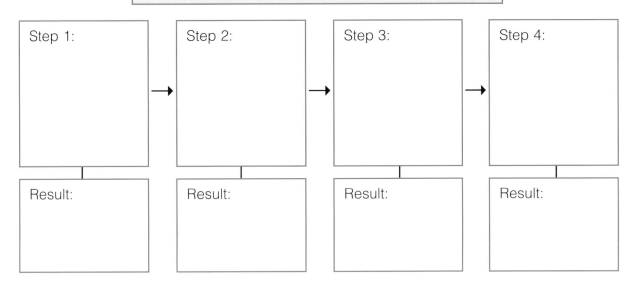

How Pfungst Discovered the Clever Hans Effect

Step 1: → Step 2: → Step 3: → Step 4:

Result: Result: Result: Result:

1. The word their in the passage refers to

(A) people
(B) horses
(C) psychologists
(D) animals

3. The word It in the passage refers to

(A) Experiment design
(B) Pfungst's discovery
(C) Involuntary cues
(D) Test subject

2. The word he in the passage refers to

(A) Pfungst
(B) the trainer
(C) Clever Hans
(D) the person asking questions

Fill in the blanks to complete the summary.

The passage discusses a psychological phenomenon called the Clever Hans Effect. It was discovered by German psychologist Oskar Pfungst when he _____ the case of a horse that could allegedly perform arithmetic and keep track of the date. In order to _____ his amazing skills, Clever Hans and his owner traveled the continent. Pfungst subjected the horse to a series of tests and discovered that the horse was actually just _____ at interpreting human body language. By being more _____ to _____ from the trainer's involuntary body language, Clever Hans was able to produce the correct answers.

Chapter 7

Sentence Simplification Questions

Necessary Skills

- Identifying the answer choice that has the same essential meaning as a highlighted sentence in a passage
- Eliminating answer choices that change the meaning in important ways or leave out essential information

Example Question

- Which of the following best expresses the essential information in the highlighted sentence? Incorrect answer choices change the meaning in important ways or leave out essential information.

Strategies

- Ensure that you understand the ways in which an answer can be incorrect. Either it contradicts a detail in the highlighted sentence, or it omits something important from the sentence.
- Be careful that your answer choice does not contradict the main argument of the paragraph in which the highlighted sentence occurs or the passage as a whole.

01 Geography

Read the following passage. Then fill in the diagram with the information that you read. `Track 40`

Rain Shadow

The hydrologic cycle is the process of evaporation and condensation in which rain is recycled until it returns to the Earth's surface in the form of precipitation. It is one of the most important cycles on the globe as it ensures a constant water supply; however, in some areas of the world, the process is interrupted, which results in the rain shadow effect.

A rain shadow is created when the hydrologic cycle is interrupted by mountains. To understand why the rain shadow effect occurs, it is important to first examine how the hydrologic cycle functions. First, water on the surface of the Earth evaporates, which is when water droplets vaporize, or turn from liquid to gas form. When evaporation occurs, the moist air rises. Near mountain ranges, as the air travels upward, it is affected by the cool temperatures of the high elevation. The air is blown toward the mountains by wind and as it cools, it begins to condense. That means the water vapor is turned into water.

However, the mountain physically obstructs the rain clouds that carry the water. Before it can reach the other side of the mountain, the water usually falls as rain or snow on the mountain; meanwhile, the leeward side of the mountain receives little to no rain. This area is called the rain shadow.

precipitation:
water that falls from clouds

droplet:
a small amount of liquid

elevation:
a height

condense:
to cause a gas to change to a liquid

obstruction:
something that blocks

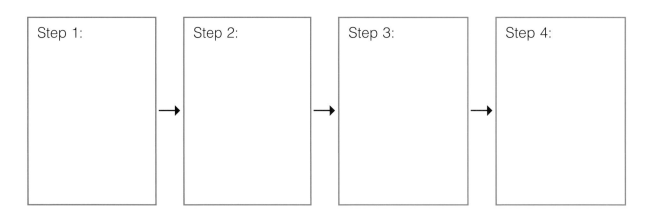

The Rain Shadow Effect

| Step 1: | Step 2: | Step 3: | Step 4: |

1. Which of the following best expresses the essential information in the highlighted sentence in paragraph 1? Incorrect answer choices change the meaning in important ways or leave out essential information.

   (A) The hydrologic cycle recycles the water on the Earth unless it occurs near a mountain, where it cannot occur.

   (B) The rain shadow effect reverses the processes of the hydrologic cycle by ensuring constant water supply.

   (C) The rain cycle helps provide water for the world except for rain shadow areas, which occur when the cycle cannot be completed.

   (D) The process of recycling water and providing water for the world is endangered by the rain shadow effect.

2. Which of the following best expresses the essential information in the highlighted sentence in paragraph 2? Incorrect answer choices change the meaning in important ways or leave out essential information.

   (A) Evaporation, the first step in the hydrologic cycle, is when water droplets turn into a gas in the form of water vapor.

   (B) If water cannot evaporate on the Earth's surface, it cannot turn into water vapor later.

   (C) When water evaporates, it causes the rain cycle to begin once again by turning water to gas.

   (D) Evaporation is the process in which water vapor turns into precipitation in the form of rain or snow.

3. Which of the following best expresses the essential information in the highlighted sentence in paragraph 3? Incorrect answer choices change the meaning in important ways or leave out essential information.

   (A) The side of the mountain facing away from the prevailing wind usually receives the most rain because it cannot travel to the other side.

   (B) The leeward side of the mountain receives the remainder of the rain that moves over the mountain.

   (C) One side of the mountain can only get water from rain that trickles down from the top of the mountain.

   (D) The mountain obstructs the passing of the precipitation, causing the leeward side to remain dry.

Fill in the blanks to complete the summary.

The passage discusses the rain shadow effect, which occurs when the hydrologic cycle is interrupted. When the water in the air evaporates, the moist air rises. When it reaches the high _____ of a mountain range, the cooler temperatures cause it to _____. Usually, water _____ fall back down to the ground as _____ after they evaporate. However, if a mountain physically _____ the rain clouds, the rain will fall before it can reach the other side. Therefore, the water never returns to that area.

---

02 Business

Read the following passage. Then fill in the diagram with the information that you read. `Track 41`

Online Auctions

The Internet has opened doors for many new and different types of businesses. One type of Internet commerce that has gained popularity in recent years is the online auction. The business model for this type of enterprise is one that allows users to bid on and purchase items over the Internet. The most popular of this business type does not actually place company-owned products up for bid. A website simply provides a marketplace for users to sell and buy products. The online auction business type has been proven extremely successful for many reasons, but the model has its limitations and drawbacks.

There are several benefits to the online auction business model. First, since it operates on the Internet, there are no time or geographic constraints. This means that commerce can occur at any time of day from any part of the world. In turn, the constant activity translates to more profits for the business. Second, the company benefits from the nature of online bidding, which involves the aspect of "winning" an auction. For many people, online auctions are much like gambling, and the prospect of winning an auction is enough to keep them coming back; therefore, online auction sites can enjoy a high level of consumer loyalty.

Despite the success of some online auction websites, the business model also has disadvantages. First, the anonymity offered to patrons of the sites often promotes the sale of stolen or counterfeit goods. With an increased awareness of the frequency of stolen goods being sold in online auctions, consumers feel less confident about bidding on products online. Second, because consumers pay for goods online, the issue of online security is important. If a company cannot ensure that personal information such as credit card numbers are protected, customers are wary of using the service.

auction:
a public sale where the person who pays the most wins the item

bid:
to offer an amount of money to buy something

constraint:
a restriction

prospect:
a possibility

anonymity:
the state of having an unknown identity

patron:
a person who uses a service

counterfeit:
fake

The Online Auction Business Model

Advantage 1:	Disadvantage 1:
Advantage 2:	Disadvantage 2:

1. Which of the following best expresses the essential information in the highlighted sentence in paragraph 1? Incorrect answer choices change the meaning in important ways or leave out essential information.

   (A) An online auction business model is severely hindered by its limitations, which is why it hasn't been used often.
   (B) The advantages of the online auction business model outweigh its disadvantages, as can be seen by its success.
   (C) The success of the online auction business model depends on the management of its limitations.
   (D) The online auction business model has both advantages and disadvantages.

2. Which of the following best expresses the essential information in the highlighted sentence in paragraph 2? Incorrect answer choices change the meaning in important ways or leave out essential information.

   (A) Online auction sites are able to draw people in by making them feel as if every purchase is a gamble.
   (B) People who enjoy gambling typically enjoy online auction sites because thcy likc to try to win.

   (C) Online auction sites can create a strong customer base because the nature of the site makes people want to use the service again.
   (D) High consumer loyalty is achieved when the customer is made to feel like their purchase is risk-free.

3. Which of the following best expresses the essential information in the highlighted sentence in paragraph 3? Incorrect answer choices change the meaning in important ways or leave out essential information.

   (A) Online auctions are at a disadvantage because criminal activity makes customers less likely to buy goods online.
   (B) The increased public awareness about the sale of stolen products on Internet auctions makes people less willing to participate in online auctions.
   (C) Consumers try to make sure that the product they have bid on is not stolen before they make a purchase.
   (D) Informed consumers will not want to bid on products if they suspect that they might be stolen goods.

Fill in the blanks to complete the summary.

The passage is about the online _____ business model, which allows people to _____ on and purchase items via the Internet. The business model has both advantages and disadvantages. The model does not have the time or geographic _____ of other businesses, and it provides high customer loyalty. However, the _____ of patrons allows for such criminal activities as the sale of stolen or _____ items.

---

03 Biology

Read the following passage. Then fill in the diagram with the information that you read. `Track 42`

Amphibians

Amphibians are a type of cold-blooded vertebrate that hatch in water and are born with gills. They are distinguishable from other animals in that they can live both in water and on land. Uncovering the evolution of amphibians has been very difficult for scientists; however, by studying fossils and modern amphibians, they have been able to guess that amphibians originated from lobe-finned fish.

Tracking amphibian evolution using fossil records is a complicated task. Very few fossils of early amphibians have been found. In fact, there is a thirty-million-year gap between fossils of the crossopterygian (a type of fish thought to be the closest ancestor of early amphibians) and the fossil of the first type of amphibian, the *Ichthyostega*. Still, by using the fossils available, scientists have tracked a number of transitional species that document the evolution of amphibians from water to land. This was done by observing the slow changes in lobe-finned fish as they developed feet-like apparatus. For example, fossils of the crossopterygian fish have primitive feet that they may have used to run along the bottom of ponds or lakes. They also have skull structures and teeth similar to early amphibians.

Fossils of the *Panderichthys* from the late Devonian period show further development of legs and amphibian-like body structures. Unlike their earlier counterparts, their bodies were flattened like amphibians. They also had straight tails, and their fins had begun to resemble feet. Fossils from the *Ichthyostega*, the first proper amphibian, show that the transition from water to land was made not too long after the *Panderichthys*. Though much larger than their modern descendants, their fully developed lung structures and feet heralded the birth of a new type of animal called the amphibian.

vertebrate:
an organism that has a backbone

gill:
an organ that allows animals to breathe underwater

transitional:
relating to the change from one form to another

apparatus:
a set of equipment for a particular use

counterpart:
something that resembles another thing

proper:
containing all definitive qualities of a thing

Species Related to Amphibian Evolution

Species 1:		Species 2:		Species 3:
Description:	→	Description:	→	Description:

1. Which of the following best expresses the essential information in the highlighted sentence in paragraph 1? Incorrect answer choices change the meaning in important ways or leave out essential information.

   (A) By studying fossils, scientists think that lobe-finned fish evolved from early amphibians.
   (B) Scientists have had trouble studying amphibian evolution because modern amphibians are so different from lobe-finned fish.
   (C) Scientists are still trying to discover how amphibians evolved from lobe-finned fish by looking for fossils of modern amphibians.
   (D) Despite the difficulty of studying amphibian evolution, scientists have determined from fossils that amphibians evolved from lobe-finned fish.

2. Which of the following best expresses the essential information in the highlighted sentence in paragraph 2? Incorrect answer choices change the meaning in important ways or leave out essential information.

   (A) The crossopterygian lived thirty million years before the first amphibian, *Ichthyostega*.
   (B) The fossils of the crossopterygians tend to be more intact than those of the first amphibian because they are older.
   (C) Judging by the fossil record, the crossopterygian and the first amphibian lived on Earth at the same time for thirty million years.
   (D) Fossils of the oldest amphibian ancestor were found thirty million years before that of the first amphibian.

3. Which of the following best expresses the essential information in the highlighted sentence in paragraph 3? Incorrect answer choices change the meaning in important ways or leave out essential information.

   (A) The large size of the *Ichthyostega* distinguishes it as the first amphibian.
   (B) Modern amphibians bear little resemblance to the first amphibian.
   (C) The *Ichthyostegas* are known to be the first type of amphibian despite their large size and lack of lungs and feet.
   (D) *Ichthyostegas* are considered the first amphibians because they had lungs and feet.

Fill in the blanks to complete the summary.

The passage is about the evolution of amphibians, which are cold-blooded animals that hatch in water and are born with _____. Few fossils of early amphibians have been found, but scientists have managed to determine some _____ species among them. From the earliest ancestor, the crossopterygian fish, scientists observed the development of feet-like _____. Later, the *Panderichthys* fish was found to have amphibian-like features, unlike its earlier _____. Finally, the fossils of the *Ichthyostega* are believed to be the first _____ amphibian.

---

04 History

Read the following passage. Then fill in the diagram with the information that you read. `Track 43`

The Roman Empire

The Roman Empire was one of the longest-lasting empires in history. It is often referred to when discussing great civilizations. It has been studied by numerous scholars, and many theories have been offered as to the reason why the Roman Empire fell in the year 476. One of these theories was proposed by anthropologist and historian Joseph Tainter. Tainter has a slightly different take on the fall of Rome, and attributes its decline to the central idea that societies collapse when they become too complex and can no longer sustain themselves.

According to Tainter, the more problems a society is posed with, the more complex they become in trying to solve the problems. But problem-solving requires resources, such as human resources, to administer and oversee the solution. It also requires monetary resources to finance the cost of the solution. As a society tries to correct itself, it continues to deplete resources until the society collapses because it can no longer maintain itself.

To support this theory, Tainter points out how the Romans dealt with the problem of limited food. The problem originated because the Romans had begun to produce less food, but the population continued to increase. At this point, according to Tainter, the society began to become more complex. Their solution was to conquer neighboring lands and take their resources, whether it was food, slaves, or metal. In solving the problem, the Roman Empire grew more multifaceted, and the solution to the problem required the extended efforts of high Roman officials, soldiers, and bureaucratic officers. In Tainter's view, the cost of solving the problem eventually caused an internal breakdown of the system. This was because the energy required to find a remedy distracted from the energy required to deal with new problems, such as invasions.

empire:
a group of countries ruled by a single person

civilization:
the state of developed human society with culture

scholar:
a person dedicated to studying a particular subject

attribute:
to believe to be a result of a cause

monetary:
relating to money

finance:
to pay for

neighboring:
next to

What Caused the Fall of Rome?

Theory:

→

Support:

1. Which of the following best expresses the essential information in the highlighted sentence in paragraph 1? Incorrect answer choices change the meaning in important ways or leave out essential information.

   (A) The decline of Rome, according to Tainter, occurred because the society could not grow or become more complex.

   (B) Tainter believes that societies like Rome fall because they cannot sustain a declining culture.

   (C) Tainter's ideas differ from other scholars in that he thinks that Rome fell because they could not sustain their increasingly complex society.

   (D) Tainter proposes that it takes knowledge of complex societies to understand why Rome fell.

2. Which of the following best expresses the essential information in the highlighted sentence in paragraph 2? Incorrect answer choices change the meaning in important ways or leave out essential information.

   (A) A society will collapse after it has exhausted all of its resources in attempts to correct problems.

   (B) When a society corrects itself, it is able to reduce its use of resources until it collapses.

   (C) A society that has fixed its problems cannot maintain itself without new resources.

   (D) The loss of resources is the main reason why societies cannot repair themselves.

3. Which of the following best expresses the essential information in the highlighted sentence in paragraph 3? Incorrect answer choices change the meaning in important ways or leave out essential information.

   (A) The Roman Empire dealt with their problems in a way that made officials work harder.

   (B) Roman bureaucracy was efficient in solving problems because they worked hard.

   (C) The Romans were demanding of their high officials because they wanted to solve too many problems.

   (D) As Romans fixed one problem, they created several others that the government could not solve.

Fill in the blanks to complete the summary.

   The passage is about Joseph Tainter's theory regarding the fall of the Roman

_____. This great _____ has been studied by many _____.

According to Tainter, Roman society was ruined because it became too complex. Complex

societies need resources to _____ the costs of solutions to their problems. In an

attempt to address their food shortage, the Romans decided to conquer _____

lands and take their resources. Eventually, the Romans only created more problems for

themselves and extended their resources until they could no longer maintain the society.

----

05 Psychology

Read the following passage. Then fill in the diagram with the information that you read. `Track 44`

The Triarchic Theory

For years, intelligence was evaluated in terms of how well a person performed mental tasks such as reading, writing, or problem-solving. Yet according to psychologist Robert Sternberg's Triarchic Theory of Human Intelligence, the key to understanding intelligence is recognizing different types. The theory proposes that intelligence is better analyzed by taking a cognitive approach, meaning that more can be learned by studying its different parts. According to Sternberg, the three components of human intelligence are: analytical, creative, and contextual.

Analytical intelligence is essentially "book smarts," since one with a high level of analytical intelligence uses skills learned in school or through books. It is the ability to solve well-defined problems that have one solution. Analytical intelligence is measured by one's reading comprehension or proficiency in academic tasks. In fact, most standardized college entrance exams test mainly analytical intelligence.

Creative intelligence refers to the cognitive ability to apply existing knowledge to new situations. In other words, it describes how well one uses previously learned skills to solve new problems. Creative intelligence also includes the ability to successfully perform unfamiliar tasks. A person with creative intelligence is often highly intuitive and artistic. A task that tests creative intelligence usually has many correct or open-ended answers.

Contextual intelligence is the ability to behave appropriately according to a given context. Sometimes referred to as "street smarts" it is not based on any type of academic learning. According to Sternberg, there are three processes for making appropriate choices. The first is adaptation, when a person changes to meet the demands of the situation. The second is shaping, when one makes changes to the environment itself. The last is selection, when a person leaves an environment to find a more suitable one. An example of this is an emigrant who leaves a place for better prospects elsewhere.

cognitive:
relating to conscious mental activity

approach:
a way of doing or solving something

proficiency:
the state of being skilled

standardized:
conforming to an approved model

intuitive:
having a deep insight

context:
a situation

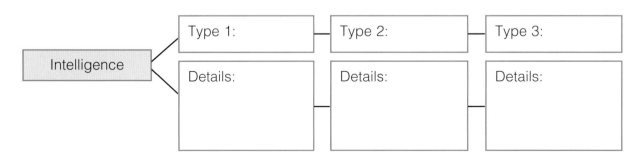

Intelligence

Type 1:

Details:

Type 2:

Details:

Type 3:

Details:

1. Which of the following best expresses the essential information in the highlighted sentence in paragraph 1? Incorrect answer choices change the meaning in important ways or leave out essential information.

   (A) Scientists stand to learn much more about human intelligence if they can formulate a better approach.
   (B) The three different parts of intelligence include a heavy emphasis on cognition.
   (C) Without employing a cognitive approach, people will never learn the extent of human intelligence.
   (D) By examining different parts of intelligence, scientists can learn more about human intelligence.

2. Which of the following best expresses the essential information in the highlighted sentence in paragraph 2? Incorrect answer choices change the meaning in important ways or leave out essential information.

   (A) Analytical intelligence only applies to people who have been educated and can use the skills they learned in school.
   (B) Learning from books is a skill that is part of analytical intelligence.

   (C) Skills learned in school or in books makes up the type of intelligence called analytical intelligence.
   (D) Analytical intelligence is promoted by schools and books because it helps people learn skills.

3. Which of the following best expresses the essential information in the highlighted sentence in paragraph 4? Incorrect answer choices change the meaning in important ways or leave out essential information.

   (A) Contextual intelligence is also called "street smarts" and does not involve analytical intelligence.
   (B) Contextual intelligence is called "street smarts" because it does not have many practical uses and is not based on academics.
   (C) Even though contextual intelligence is referred to as "street smarts," it has little to do with intelligence or academic knowledge.
   (D) Academic learning is also called "street smarts" because it is not based on traditional intelligence.

Fill in the blanks to complete the summary.

The passage is about Robert Sterberg's Triarchic Theory of Human Intelligence. His _____ studies three components of intelligence: analytical, creative, and contextual. Analytical intelligence is measured by _____ in academic tasks, and is often determined through the use of _____ tests. Creative intelligence is how well a person can apply known skills to new situations. Often, creatively intelligent people are quite _____. Contextual intelligence is the ability to behave appropriately in any given _____.

----

06 | Anthropology

Read the following passage. Then fill in the diagram with the information that you read. `Track 45`

The Spread of Culture

Cultural diffusion occurs when aspects or traits from one culture are spread and incorporated into another culture. It is a natural process that does not involve a country forcing its traditions and culture onto another, as in assimilation. Three recognized modes of cultural diffusion are direct contact, intermediate contact, and stimulus diffusion.

Direct contact diffusion occurs when one culture directly borrows from another. This is usually facilitated by close proximity; in other words, when two countries are located near each other, they are more likely to experience direct contact diffusion. For example, the game of hockey, a favorite national pastime in Canada, is now popular in the United States. The United States has also influenced Canadian culture by popularizing baseball in the northern country.

Intermediate contact diffusion is when parts of a culture spread through an intermediary, or "middleman." In the past, intermediaries were merchant sailors or missionaries traveling to distant countries who returned with cultural treasures. For example, anthropologists believe that soldiers were instrumental in the spread of culture during the Middle Ages. The Knights Templar and the Knights of St. John traveled between North Africa and Europe. As they did so, they spread different aspects of their respective cultures. Furthermore, it can be argued that today, the Internet is a primary intermediary for cultural diffusion as it connects people from all over the world.

The last type of cultural diffusion is stimulus diffusion. This occurs when the knowledge of a certain trait is enough to spur the creation of an equal trait or aspect in another culture. Without direct contact, this tends to be an interpretation of the culture's traits rather than an exact replica. Take the case of the arrival of Europeans in North America. A Cherokee Indian named Sequoya noted that the Europeans had a writing system. Without directly adopting the English system, Sequoya developed a completely unique writing system for his people.

incorporate:
to include something

assimilation:
the process in which a group takes on cultural and other traits of a larger group

mode:
a way of doing something

intermediate:
being between two things

instrumental:
important in causing something to happen

spur:
to encourage

replica:
an exact copy of something

Cultural Diffusion

Type 1:

Explanation:

Type 2:	Explanation:

Type 3:	Explanation:

1. Which of the following best expresses the essential information in the highlighted sentence in paragraph 1? Incorrect answer choices change the meaning in important ways or leave out essential information.

(A) Cultural diffusion is when one culture loses its characteristics.

(B) A culture incorporating immigrants from another is referred to as cultural diffusion.

(C) The acceptance of characteristics of one culture into another is known as cultural diffusion.

(D) The diffusion of one culture into another usually results in war.

2. Which of the following best expresses the essential information in the highlighted sentence in paragraph 2? Incorrect answer choices change the meaning in important ways or leave out essential information.

(A) A country's location determines how much diffusion occurs there.

(B) It is probable that neighboring countries will have direct contact diffusion.

(C) Direct contact diffusion can only occur between countries that are in very close proximity.

(D) Countries that are located close together have facilities to help deal with direct contact diffusion.

3. Which of the following best expresses the essential information in the highlighted sentence in paragraph 3? Incorrect answer choices change the meaning in important ways or leave out essential information.

(A) Supporters of the Internet think that it enables cultural diffusion.

(B) It is unknown if the Internet affects intermediate contact diffusion.

(C) The Internet puts people in contact in order to promote diffusion.

(D) The Internet is a modern agent of intermediate contact diffusion.

Fill in the blanks to complete the summary.

The passage discusses cultural diffusion, when aspects of a culture are _____ into another. There are three different _____ of cultural diffusion. Direct contact diffusion occurs when one culture takes on aspects of a culture that it has contact with. _____ contact diffusion is when the spread of a culture happens through a "middleman." Stimulus diffusion is when the knowledge of a certain trait _____ the invention of a similar trait in another culture, though it may not be an exact _____.

Chapter 8 | Text Insertion Questions

Necessary Skills

- Understanding the logic of a reading passage and grammatical connections between sentences

Example Question

- Look at the four squares [■] that indicate where the following sentence could be added to the passage.

[You will see a sentence in bold here.]

Where would the sentence best fit?

Strategies

- Try inserting the bolded sentence in place of each square.
- Pay attention to both the structure of the bolded sentence and the logic of its placement.
- Watch for logical connecting words as they can give important clues about where the sentence should be placed.
- Ensure that the bolded sentence connects logically to both the sentence preceding it and the sentence following it.

01 Biology

Read the following passage. Then fill in the diagram with the information that you read. `Track 46`

Fungi

■ **A)** While fungi can be a nuisance due to their destructive capabilities, the members of the kingdom fungi have many attributes that make them vital to environments. ■ **B)** In fact, ecosystems rely on fungi to remain clean and healthy. ■ **C)** Fungi, such as mushrooms, molds, and yeasts, have two functions in preserving the health of ecosystems. ■ **D)**

Unlike other plants that create their own food through the process of photosynthesis, fungi obtain nutrients through hosts. Hosts are the plants or animals on which they live. ● **A)** In the process of decomposition, fungi break down organic material from these hosts into inorganic material. This material can be returned as nutrients back into the environment. ● **B)** Without these nutrients, the soil would not be able to support new life, and all life in the environment would eventually die. ● **C)** Thus, through their destructive capabilities, fungi allow life to persist. ● **D)**

◆ **A)** Fungi also exhibit reproductive behavior that is unique to their kingdom. ◆ **B)** Fungi reproduce through the use of spores, which are microscopic particles that the fungi release into the air. As the spores land on a habitable area, such as a damp patch in a forest, they begin to reproduce themselves. This sends even more spores into the air. ◆ **C)** In fact, mold, which is one of the fastest reproducing fungi, is used in the creation of many antibiotics due to its ability to reproduce so quickly. This allows the medicine to be easily manufactured in large quantities. ◆ **D)**

nuisance:
a source of annoyance or trouble

capability:
the quality of being able to do something

exhibit:
to show something

microscopic:
too small to be seen without the use of a microscope

habitable:
able to be lived in

antibiotic:
a medicine used to destroy bacteria

Fungi

Characteristic 1:

→ Role:

Characteristic 2:

→ Role:

1. Look at the four squares [■] that indicate where the following sentence could be added to the passage.

   These roles allow fungi to be put to important and surprising uses.

   Where would the sentence best fit?

   (A) First square
   (B) Second square
   (C) Third square
   (D) Fourth square

2. Look at the four circles [●] that indicate where the following sentence could be added to the passage.

   For example, fungi can decompose dead leaves, which in turn will return the nutrients in those leaves to the soil.

   Where would the sentence best fit?

   (A) First circle
   (B) Second circle
   (C) Third circle
   (D) Fourth circle

3. Look at the four diamonds [◆] that indicate where the following sentence could be added to the passage.

   This behavior allows fungi to spread quickly in an environment and reach new areas in which they had not previously been present.

   Where would the sentence best fit?

   (A) First diamond
   (B) Second diamond
   (C) Third diamond
   (D) Fourth diamond

Fill in the blanks to complete the summary.

According to the passage, although fungi can be a(n) _____, they are vital to ecosystems. Despite their destructive _____, fungi help to decompose organic matter so that nutrients will be returned to the environment. In addition, fungi _____ reproductive behavior through the use of spores. Once the spores find a(n) _____ area, they reproduce very quickly. This reproductive ability has led to their use in the development of _____ in modern medicine.

Read the following passage. Then fill in the diagram with the information that you read. `Track 47`

Product Stewardship

■ **A)** Trash disposal is a problem that cannot be solved easily. The issue has led to the suggestion of various solutions. ■ **B)** Previous waste reduction efforts focused on specific groups—consumers or the government, for example—and their parts in solving the problem. However, a new theory called product stewardship instead looks toward cooperation between all groups involved in a product's life. ■ **C)** The theory suggests that environmental protection plans must be implemented at each stage of a product's life cycle: from its conception to its eventual disposal. ■ **D)**

Product stewardship recognizes a manufacturer's ability to reduce a product's environmental impact in a number of ways. First, manufacturers are rethinking the way in which they package their products. ● **A)** Thus, packaging is increasingly being produced with recyclability and non-toxicity in mind. ● **B)** Manufacturers are also actively promoting recycling of their products using product labels. ● **C)** Some battery companies have implemented programs that are aimed at reducing a battery's environmental impact. ● **D)**

Many retailers are now participating in programs to reduce the impact of the products that they sell. Retailers are in an important position because they act as the mediators between manufacturers and consumers. ◆ **A)** In addition, retailers can create their own recycling programs that allow consumers to more easily execute the recycling plans suggested by manufacturers. ◆ **B)** For example, some office supply retailers have instated recycling programs for used ink cartridges. ◆ **C)** These programs motivate consumers to bring back used cartridges in return for a small payment. Then, the cartridges are sent back to the printer company so they may be reused. ◆ **D)**

While much of the government's role has been to foster recycling, many programs have been created to allow a more direct role in environmental protection. One such program has been started in some US states. It attempts to encourage the recycling of cans and bottles. In these states, consumers are charged a container deposit for each recyclable can or bottle they purchase. This fee is generally five or ten cents. Then, consumers can get this deposit back if they take the container to a recycling center.

implement:
to set up; to establish

life cycle:
the complete process of change and development during the useful life of something

toxicity:
the degree to which a substance is poisonous

mediator:
a link between two people or groups

execute:
to put a plan into action

instate:
to establish

foster:
to encourage; to allow

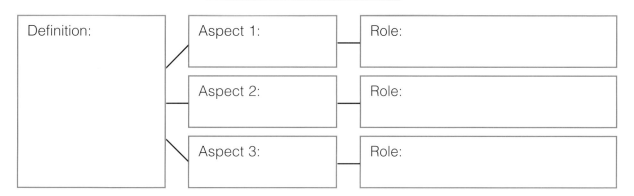

1. Look at the four squares [■] that indicate where the following sentence could be added to the passage.

   Through these plans, a product's environmental impact can be reduced.

   Where would the sentence best fit?

   (A) First square
   (B) Second square
   (C) Third square
   (D) Fourth square

2. Look at the four circles [●] that indicate where the following sentence could be added to the passage.

   In addition to using such visual reminders, manufacturers have even begun paying to recycle their products.

Where would the sentence best fit?

(A) First circle
(B) Second circle
(C) Third circle
(D) Fourth circle

3. Look at the four diamonds [◆] that indicate where the following sentence could be added to the passage.

   For this reason, many retailers aid manufacturers in transmitting their messages of recycling to consumers.

   Where would the sentence best fit?

   (A) First diamond
   (B) Second diamond
   (C) Third diamond
   (D) Fourth diamond

Fill in the blanks to complete the summary.

The passage discusses the concept of product stewardship. It encourages environmental

protection plans that are _____ throughout a product's entire life cycle.

Manufacturers have begun using new packaging that is recyclable and non-_____.

Retailers are also acting as _____ between manufacturers and consumers. They

are also _____ recycling programs. Lastly, state governments are

_____ recycling through many programs, such as the container deposit program.

----

03 | Astronomy

Read the following passage. Then fill in the diagram with the information that you read. `Track 48`

Venus's Runaway Greenhouse Effect

Earth and Venus are quite different atmospherically despite their relative proximity in our solar system. ■ **A)** The most striking difference is the atmospheric temperature on Venus. It is about five times the average temperature on Earth. ■ **B)** In addition, the atmosphere of Venus is about 96.5 percent carbon dioxide, with almost no water vapor at all. ■ **C)** The answer proposed by many astronomers is that Venus experienced what they refer to as a runaway greenhouse effect. ■ **D)**

● **A)** Because Venus is not close enough to the sun for its solar proximity to explain the planet's heat, researchers developed the theory of the runaway greenhouse effect to explain the temperature. ● **B)** Just as greenhouse gases serve to heat Earth, they do the same to Venus. However, the effect is exacerbated on Venus due to the planet's high concentration of carbon dioxide. In essence, the carbon dioxide acts as a barrier. It prevents the infrared radiation of the sun from escaping the atmosphere. ● **C)** While one can imagine Earth as having a thin barrier that traps solar radiation, Venus contains a very thick barrier due to its atmospheric makeup. ● **D)**

The process that prevented oceans from appearing on Venus must be traced back to Venus's formation. It is very likely that Venus contained water during the time just after its formation. ◆ **A)** Due to the heat, clouds never produced rain, and water vapor remained in the atmosphere. ◆ **B)** Its presence served much the same purpose as carbon dioxide. Therefore, as more water vapor was introduced into the atmosphere, the surface temperature on Venus rose. ◆ **C)** This process would then have "run away." In other words, the problem reached such a level that any liquid water evaporated. Once in the atmosphere, this water vapor escaped as it was broken down by the sun's radiation. Then, even more carbon dioxide entered the atmosphere. ◆ **D)**

proximity:
nearness

runaway:
out of control

greenhouse effect:
the heating of a planet due to the inability of heat to leave the atmosphere

serve:
to have the function of

exacerbate:
to make worse

concentration:
density

The Runaway Greenhouse Effect

Cause 1:	Effect:

Cause 2:	Effect:

1. Look at the four squares [■] that indicate where the following sentence could be added to the passage.

   These factors suggest an effect that, at some point in its history, caused Venus to develop its current atmosphere.

   Where would the sentence best fit?

   (A) First square
   (B) Second square
   (C) Third square
   (D) Fourth square

2. Look at the four circles [●] that indicate where the following sentence could be added to the passage.

   Thus, a lower amount of heat is allowed to escape Venus, causing the temperature to remain constantly hot.

   Where would the sentence best fit?

   (A) First circle
   (B) Second circle
   (C) Third circle
   (D) Fourth circle

3. Look at the four diamonds [◆] that indicate where the following sentence could be added to the passage.

   However, due to the heat caused by the greenhouse effect, liquid water that might have existed slowly began to evaporate into water vapor.

   Where would the sentence best fit?

   (A) First diamond
   (B) Second diamond
   (C) Third diamond
   (D) Fourth diamond

Fill in the blanks to complete the summary.

The passage discusses the _____ greenhouse effect on Venus.
Greenhouse gases _____ to heat both Earth and Venus. However, their atmospheres
are much different despite their relative _____ to each other. Venus's high
_____ of carbon dioxide acts as a barrier. This _____ the
heating effect by preventing the sun's infrared radiation from escaping Venus's atmosphere.
The heat caused by the gases allowed water to evaporate and escape the atmosphere,
which is why oceans never formed on Venus.

04 | History

Read the following passage. Then fill in the diagram with the information that you read. `Track 49`

Frederick Law Olmsted

In the mid-1800s, American cities were experiencing rapid population growth. At this time, the idea of beautification of the urban landscape became an important consideration in city planning. ■ **A)** The pioneer of the design and construction of preserved public space was Frederick Law Olmsted. ■ **B)** He is considered to be the leading landscape architect following the Civil War period. He effected many changes in the conception of public space. ■ **C)** The primary purpose of public parks suggested by Olmsted was to create a quiet, passive, open space—a kind of sanctuary from the bustle of the city. ■ **D)** Olmsted also made public space accessible to everyone, rather than a specific group of people.

The need for public spaces arose from the realization that cities lacked a cohesive balance of areas for work, play, and living. ● **A)** Cities had become crowded and stressful, and city planners recognized the desire of citizens for an escape from city life. ● **B)** Thus, Olmsted planned his park with escape in mind. ● **C)** In fact, his goal was to create a space that differed from New York City as much as possible while remaining integrated in the city's overall structure. ● **D)** Olmsted planned the park very carefully, though the end result looked very natural, as if it had always been a part of New York City.

◆ **A)** While many previous public spaces catered to specific groups of people, Olmsted planned Central Park as a truly public space. ◆ **B)** Many earlier parks had been similar in design, though they catered either to the wealthy or to members of the government. ◆ **C)** Even in the mid-19th century, public space was not truly public. Instead, its use by the homeless, the poor, and the young was discouraged. ◆ **D)** Olmsted, however, wanted public spaces to be available to all people. Thus, he created Central Park to be truly centralized in New York City. Its location in the middle of the city ensured that traveling to the park was practical for all citizens.

beautification:
the improvement of the visual appeal of something

pioneer:
someone who introduces a new idea

effect:
to make happen

sanctuary:
a place to find rest and relaxation

bustle:
chaotic activity

cohesive:
connecting parts in a practical way

cater:
to provide something that is desired

Olmsted and Public Space

Topic:	Point 1:	Explanation:
	Point 2:	Explanation:

1. Look at the four squares [■] that indicate where the following sentence could be added to the passage.

   The most notable of these transformations is Central Park in New York City.

   Where would the sentence best fit?

   (A) First square
   (B) Second square
   (C) Third square
   (D) Fourth square

2. Look at the four circles [●] that indicate where the following sentence could be added to the passage.

   The motivation behind New York's Central Park reflected this desire.

Where would the sentence best fit?

(A) First circle
(B) Second circle
(C) Third circle
(D) Fourth circle

3. Look at the four diamonds [◆] that indicate where the following sentence could be added to the passage.

   For example, King Louis XIV of 17th-century France created many beautiful parks, though they were intended for him and his royal counterparts.

   Where would the sentence best fit?

   (A) First diamond
   (B) Second diamond
   (C) Third diamond
   (D) Fourth diamond

Fill in the blanks to complete the summary.

The passage discusses the changes in public spaces _____ by landscape architect Frederick Law Olmsted. He realized that cities lacked a(n) _____ balance of places in which to work, play, and live. Olmsted planned Central Park in New York around the idea that people needed a(n) _____ in order to escape the _____ of city life. While previous public spaces had _____ to certain groups of people, Olmsted wanted Central Park to be accessible to all members of the public.

05 Psychology

Read the following passage. Then fill in the diagram with the information that you read. `Track 50`

Selective Attention Theory

Why do people focus their attention on particular elements of their surroundings while completely ignoring others? Selective attention theories propose answers to this question. ■ **A)** Most people have been in a situation where their attention was focused on a difficult issue, such as a challenging homework problem, and became inattentive to other stimuli in the environment. ■ **B)** Selective attention theories, then, attempt to describe how one can focus on a single consuming issue and ignore other stimuli. ■ **C)** These theories can be separated into two distinct categories: filter theories and attentional resource theories. ■ **D)**

Donald Broadbent proposed the first filter theory in 1958. It would become the basis for subsequent filter theories. ● **A)** In his theory, Broadbent suggested that humans begin to filter information immediately after it is heard. ● **B)** For example, Broadbent believed that humans disregard the chatter in a busy room if it has no relevance to their current train of thought. ● **C)** Therefore, the brain must first process the information and regard certain stimuli (one's name, for example) as having higher importance. ● **D)** The brain, then, processes anything that enters through the ear. However, not all information enters the consciousness of the subject. Essentially, the brain filters anything that is unfamiliar. A familiar name or voice can redirect one's attention.

In contrast, attentional resource theories state that attention is dependent not upon filters but upon a fixed amount of attention that one can devote to tasks. ◆ **A)** Imagine attention as a percentage. Now, imagine that at any given time, one can devote one hundred percent of his or her attention to a given task. ◆ **B)** Returning to the example of the crowded room, a person would have to divide his or her attention according to all stimuli in the room. ◆ **C)** This person might devote, for example, seventy percent of his or her attention to a conversation with a friend. ◆ **D)** Thus, thirty percent of his or her attentional resources would be available for other tasks. These tasks could be listening to other conversations in the room or even thinking about a baseball game. If he or she wanted to devote more attention to the conversation, attentional resources would have to be redirected from another task.

selective:
characterized by the ability to make choices

stimulus:
something that causes a person to perform an action

subsequent:
next in a series

disregard:
to ignore

relevance:
the relation to a current topic or matter

redirect:
to move from one place to another

devote:
to commit to a particular purpose

| Selective Attention Theories |

| Theory 1: | → | Explanation: | → | Example: |

| Theory 2: | → | Explanation: | → | Example: |

1. Look at the four squares [■] that indicate where the following sentence could be added to the passage.

   These might include a conversation in the same room or the noise from a construction site outside.

   Where would the sentence best fit?

   (A) First square
   (B) Second square
   (C) Third square
   (D) Fourth square

2. Look at the four circles [●] that indicate where the following sentence could be added to the passage.

   However, later filter theorists recognized that people will still respond to their name in a crowded room, even if it was not a part of their current conversation.

   Where would the sentence best fit?

   (A) First circle
   (B) Second circle
   (C) Third circle
   (D) Fourth circle

3. Look at the four diamonds [◆] that indicate where the following sentence could be added to the passage.

   This attention can be thought of in numerical terms.

   Where would the sentence best fit?

   (A) First diamond
   (B) Second diamond
   (C) Third diamond
   (D) Fourth diamond

Fill in the blanks to complete the summary.

The passage discusses _____ attention theories, which try to determine why people focus their attention in different ways. Filter theories say that the brain filters out unwanted information. For example, a person _____ conversations in a room if they have no _____ to his or her thoughts. One's brain can filter unfamiliar information and _____ attention to familiar names or voices. Attentional resource theories describe attention as a fixed amount to divide according to how much attention one wants to pay to something. A person can _____ a certain amount of attention to certain stimuli.

---

06 Literature

Read the following passage. Then fill in the diagram with the information that you read. `Track 51`

Allegory

■ **A)** Authors use many storytelling techniques to give the basic events of their story a deeper meaning. ■ **B)** In an allegory, the author uses metaphor to such an extent that the entire story becomes an extended metaphor for something completely unrelated to the events of the story itself. ■ **C)** Allegory can have many uses, though it is most often used either to provide another way to understand a difficult concept or to represent a story in a new, entertaining way. ■ **D)**

Plato's allegory of the cave is an example of using an allegory in order to help readers understand the concepts being discussed. ● **A)** Plato believed in a world of forms, in which everything existed in its "real" state. ● **B)** Realizing that these concepts are difficult to understand, Plato wrote the allegory of the cave in his philosophical work *The Republic*. In it, Plato uses an extended metaphor to explain his concepts. ● **C)** The allegory involves prisoners chained up in a cave who can look only at the wall of the cave and cannot turn around to view the entrance. The prisoners can see the shadows of the activity happening outside, and they mistake these shadows for reality. ● **D)** However, one prisoner manages to escape his bondage and leave the cave. He can now see the real world instead of shadows. The allegory, then, is attempting to explain philosophical knowledge. The prisoners represent the public, who can only see the representations of the forms (the shadows on the wall). Only by escaping the cave can one see the real representation of the world as philosophers do.

◆ **A)** In addition, writers use allegories to create a new telling of a familiar story. An example is *Animal Farm* by George Orwell. ◆ **B)** Orwell wanted to write a story about the political situation in the 1940s. ◆ **C)** Instead, Orwell placed his story in the world of a farm of animals. Many of the characters were pigs, horses, and donkeys. In the story, the animals stage a revolution and evict the humans from their farm. However, the animals soon find that they are not fit to govern the farm themselves, and their situation turns into a disaster. Thus, Orwell's story is literally about animals taking over a farm. ◆ **D)** However, the allegorical meaning of the story describes Orwell's viewpoint on a popular topic in 1940s politics. In fact, most allegories can be understood literally, according to the events that transpire in the book, and figuratively, in terms of what those events represent.

metaphor:
figurative language; a concept that is used to represent an unrelated idea

bondage:
the state of being restrained

stage:
to plan and carry out

evict:
to put out from a building

fit:
well suited

transpire:
to happen

figuratively:
using a metaphor; not literally

Allegory

Definition:	Role 1:	Example:
	Role 2:	Example:

1. Look at the four squares [■] that indicate where the following sentence could be added to the passage.

   One such literary technique is called allegory.

   Where would the sentence best fit?

   (A) First square
   (B) Second square
   (C) Third square
   (D) Fourth square

2. Look at the four circles [●] that indicate where the following sentence could be added to the passage.

   Everything in our world, however, was just a representation of the real version of the object in the world of the forms.

   Where would the sentence best fit?

   (A) First circle
   (B) Second circle
   (C) Third circle
   (D) Fourth circle

3. Look at the four diamonds [◆] that indicate where the following sentence could be added to the passage.

   However, had he written about politics directly, the story would have been simply a telling of current events.

   Where would the sentence best fit?

   (A) First diamond
   (B) Second diamond
   (C) Third diamond
   (D) Fourth diamond

Fill in the blanks to complete the summary.

The passage discusses the use of allegory in literature. Allegory is used as an extended metaphor for two reasons. The first is to explain difficult concepts. For example, Plato uses the _____ of prisoners to explain philosophical knowledge. The second purpose of allegory is to tell a familiar story in a new way. For instance, in George Orwell's *Animal Farm,* farm animals _____ a revolution to _____ humans from their farm. They soon discover that they are not _____ to run the farm themselves. The story's events _____ represent the political situation of Orwell's time.

Vocabulary Review 2

Instructions: Choose the best word or phrase to complete each sentence.

1. The article was written by a famous _____ from a university in Australia.
   - (A) ancestor
   - (B) scholar
   - (C) pioneer
   - (D) barrier

2. The people in the crowd had to _____ their necks in order to see the fireworks display overhead.
   - (A) precede
   - (B) foster
   - (C) manipulate
   - (D) crane

3. The new law will be put into effect when the council _____ next month.
   - (A) convenes
   - (B) renders
   - (C) postulates
   - (D) serves

4. When I said that I was so hungry I could eat a horse, I was speaking _____.
   - (A) passively
   - (B) inevitably
   - (C) actively
   - (D) figuratively

5. Side effects of this medication may include headaches, _____, and nausea.
   - (A) weariness
   - (B) diversity
   - (C) exertion
   - (D) drowsiness

6. The maritime museum features a miniature _____ of the Titanic on display.
   - (A) replica
   - (B) fossil
   - (C) counterpart
   - (D) mechanism

7. Some slimming drugs are designed to _____ your appetite so you do not feel hungry.
   - (A) surpass
   - (B) isolate
   - (C) suppress
   - (D) implement

8. The _____ that were caused by the earthquake were so strong that the pictures on the wall crashed to the floor.
   - (A) migrations
   - (B) tremors
   - (C) stimulus
   - (D) mediators

Instructions: Choose the word or phrase closest in meaning to the underlined part of each sentence.

9. Hikers may have trouble breathing once they reach the mountain's peak due to the extreme <u>height</u>.
   - (A) elevation
   - (B) composition
   - (C) variation
   - (D) proximity

10. You are not allowed to <u>bring in</u> fruits, vegetables, or meats when you travel to another country.

(A) import
(B) cater
(C) evict
(D) repel

11. To ensure fairness, the teacher should <u>try not to</u> call on the same student over and over during class.

(A) adorn
(B) avoid
(C) ignore
(D) spur

12. It is <u>thought</u> that about 44,000 Americans die each year in hospitals as a result of preventable medical errors.

(A) incorporated
(B) instated
(C) disregarded
(D) estimated

13. Because the main <u>road</u> to the lake was blocked by a fallen tree, we had to find an alternate road to the cabin.

(A) cue
(B) terrain
(C) route
(D) sanctuary

14. My health is the <u>main</u> reason behind my choice to quit smoking.

(A) apparent
(B) primary
(C) proper
(D) intuitive

15. The restaurant's policy not to permit pets inside is strictly <u>imposed</u>.

(A) enforced
(B) stationary
(C) confirmed
(D) cohesive

Instructions: Write the missing words. Use the words below to fill in the blanks.

fossils	preserved	devote
instrumental	identifying	

Paleontology is the study of the life of Earth's history as reflected in fossil records. From the Greek "paleo" and "ology," paleontology literally means the study of ancient beings.
16. _____ are the remains or traces of organisms, such as plants, animals, fungi, and bacteria that lived in the geological past and are **17.** _____ in the Earth's crust. Paleontologists **18.** _____ much of their time to digging up and
19. _____ fossils. Many of the life forms that paleontologists study are extinct. These fossils are **20.** _____ in providing us with information about life that existed on Earth long before humans.

Instructions: Match the words that are similar in meaning.

21. exacerbate (A) city
22. subsequent (B) worsen
23. counterfeit (C) fake
24. metropolis (D) adjust
25. regulate (E) following

Mini Test 2

01 Zoology

Read the passage and answer the questions.   `Track 52`

Animal Communication

Animals have their own methods of communication, whether they communicate through body language or through rudimentary grunts and yelps. For example, giraffes press their necks together to convey affection. Dolphins communicate with unique whistling noises. However, can animals be taught to communicate using a form of human language? Many scientists believe that chimpanzees are so genetically similar to humans that chimps can indeed be taught to communicate with human language. They have spent years conducting research to prove their theory.

To further explore the theory, the Language Research Center in Atlanta, Georgia, has been performing language tests on chimpanzees since the 1970s. ■ **A)** The most successful finding occurred with a chimp named Kanzi. Researchers had been working with an older primate when they discovered that Kanzi had learned the method of communication they had been teaching the other chimpanzee. ■ **B)** Using a keyboard with geometric symbols that stood for certain words, Kanzi developed a vocabulary of two hundred words. ■ **C)** Kanzi used the keyboard and some <u>gestures</u> to communicate basic sentences. ■ **D)** He even seemed to understand instructions. Scientists were astounded when Kanzi was instructed to "give the dog a shot." Kanzi picked up a hypodermic needle and injected a stuffed toy dog.

While Kanzi's achievement was important, another chimp would later make a breakthrough that showed true progress in the scientists' attempts. ● **A)** A chimp named Panbanisha had been taught to communicate with a keyboard similar to the one Kanzi used. ● **B)** One morning, Panbanisha grabbed the keyboard and repeatedly typed in "fight," "mad," and "Austin." ● **C)** Another chimpanzee named Austin lived in a building near Panbanisha. That morning, Austin had had a loud disagreement with another chimpanzee. ● **D)** It appeared that Panbanisha had overheard his fight and decided to talk about it with the researcher.

Panbanisha's ability to create a crude sentence proved what researchers had hoped—that chimpanzees could be taught to communicate about something more than just their basic needs. Panbanisha's breakthrough showed that chimps could communicate about things around them or, in this instance, could communicate gossip. Up to this point, researchers had not seen such communicative similarities between animals and humans. The research with Panbanisha proved that chimpanzees can be trained to communicate with people through language. While this is a long way from having true conversation, the evidence shows that animals can use human language to communicate on more than just a basic level with people.

▶ **gesture** *an action intended to communicate feelings or intentions*

1. The word rudimentary in the passage is closest in meaning to

   (A) peaceful   (B) basic
   (C) plain   (D) authentic

2. Which of the following best expresses the essential information in the highlighted sentence in paragraph 1? Incorrect answer choices change the meaning in important ways or leave out essential information.

   (A) Because chimps and people are able to communicate using human language, they have become genetically alike.
   (B) The genetic connection between people and chimps allows them to communicate with one another through human language.
   (C) Genetic links between chimpanzees and people have led scientists to think that chimps can communicate using human language.
   (D) It is genetically likely that chimpanzees and people will communicate with each other.

3. The word their in the paragraph 1 refers to

   (A) humans'   (B) chimpanzees'
   (C) animals'   (D) scientists'

4. Look at the four squares [■] that indicate where the following sentence could be added to the passage.

   Like human children, Kanzi learned communicative skills through imitation.

   Where would the sentence best fit?

   (A) First square
   (B) Second square
   (C) Third square
   (D) Fourth square

5. Look at the four circles [●] that indicate where the following sentence could be added to the passage.

   Upon investigation, the research team discovered what the chimp was trying to communicate.

   Where would the sentence best fit?

   (A) First circle
   (B) Second circle
   (C) Third circle
   (D) Fourth circle

6. The word his in the passage refers to

   (A) Austin's   (B) Panbanisha's
   (C) researcher's   (D) Kanzi's

7. The word crude in the passage is closest in meaning to

   (A) short   (B) simple
   (C) offensive   (D) unprocessed

8. Which of the following best expresses the essential information in the highlighted sentence in paragraph 4? Incorrect answer choices change the meaning in important ways or leave out essential information.

   (A) Scientific proof indicates that animals communicate with people using true human language.
   (B) Human language allows for meaningful communication to occur between animals and people.
   (C) Because of scientific research, people can now communicate with animals using human language.
   (D) Scientific proof reveals that some meaningful communication between animals and people is possible.

02 Linguistics

Read the passage and answer the questions. ` Track 53 `

Dying Languages

It is thought that at one point, there were over 200,000 languages in use around the world. Today, there are approximately 6,800 living or actively spoken languages in existence. This number includes obscure languages spoken by only a handful of people in remote parts of the world. Even with the immense number of languages in active use, researchers in the field of linguistics feel there are literally hundreds of languages in danger of extinction at a rate faster than that of many endangered animals. ■ **A)** In fact, linguists estimate that one language falls out of use about every two weeks. ■ **B)** The circumstances surrounding the disappearance of languages can be attributed to different causes. ■ **C)** Many of these languages also have no written form, which makes them particularly susceptible to being lost and forgotten. ■ **D)**

Several cultures of the world are seeing a decline in their native tongues. ● **A)** Australia, a very language-rich country, has already lost many Aborigine languages. Several more have only one or two people still alive who can recall their specific intonations and word meanings. ● **B)** A similar situation is seen in North America. Native Americans in several areas have tribal languages spoken on reservations that are becoming obsolete. ● **C)** The absence of those with knowledge of ancient languages leaves no one who can articulate the words spoken by their ancestors. ● **D)**

Many other countries are seeing indigenous languages being choked out by the prevailing languages. The Amazon region in South America has seen the rise of Spanish and Portuguese as the languages of choice. The languages spoken by many people in remote regions are no longer being learned by new generations. The reduction of minority languages in Siberia can be directly attributed to the Russian national government, which established a policy that forces speakers of minority languages to use only the declared national and regional languages. This decreases the use of minority languages in Siberia and will eventually lead to language extinction.

Of the thousands of languages still in existence, only eighty-three are considered to have global influence. These are used by the vast majority of people in the world. Though several groups have been working to capture and preserve endangered languages through written and auditory means, most will be lost to daily use forever. Their regression is viewed as a great loss of cultural understanding and heritage from the past.

▸ **obscure** *unknown to most people*

1. The word remote in the passage is closest in meaning to

   (A) reserved
   (B) isolated
   (C) available
   (D) dominant

2. Which of the following best expresses the essential information in the highlighted sentence in paragraph 1? Incorrect answer choices change the meaning in important ways or leave out essential information.

   (A) As many languages are in danger of being lost, so too are many animals at risk of becoming extinct.
   (B) Although there are many languages in existence, they are becoming lost more often than endangered animals.
   (C) Although many languages are in use, hundreds are at risk of being lost faster than many endangered animals.
   (D) While many animals face extinction, linguists feel that the danger of dying languages is greater.

3. Look at the four squares [■] that indicate where the following sentence could be added to the passage.

   These causes range from the death of the speakers to the more gradual decrease in use as people learn more widely accepted languages.

   Where would the sentence best fit?

   (A) First square
   (B) Second square
   (C) Third square
   (D) Fourth square

4. Look at the four circles [●] that indicate where the following sentence could be added to the passage.

   This is due to the death of the older members who grew up speaking the language.

Where would the sentence best fit?

   (A) First circle
   (B) Second circle
   (C) Third circle
   (D) Fourth circle

5. Which of the following best expresses the essential information in the highlighted sentence in paragraph 3? Incorrect answer choices change the meaning in important ways or leave out essential information.

   (A) The Russian government is responsible for a policy under which many people cannot use their own native language.
   (B) Minority languages are illegal in Siberia due to the government's policy that favors speakers of the national language.
   (C) Russia's government introduced a rule favoring the use of local languages in favor of little-used languages.
   (D) Speakers of Siberia's national language are part of a policy made by the government seeking to reduce minority languages.

6. The word This in the passage refers to

   (A) National government
   (B) Policy
   (C) Minority language
   (D) National language

7. The word most in the passage refers to

   (A) languages
   (B) people
   (C) countries
   (D) groups

8. The word regression in the passage is closest in meaning to

   (A) decline
   (B) slump
   (C) failure
   (D) collapse

Chapter 9

Prose Summary Questions

Necessary Skills

- Recognizing the organization and relative importance of information presented in a passage
- Understanding and locating specific points in a passage key to the gist of a passage as a whole
- Organizing information presented in a passage into a mental outline

Example Question

- An introductory sentence for a brief summary of the passage is provided below. Complete the summary by selecting the THREE answer choices that express the most important ideas in the passage. Some sentences do not belong in the summary because they express ideas that are not presented in the passage or are minor ideas in the passage. ***This question is worth 2 points.***

  [You will see a sentence in bold here.]

Strategies

- Distinguish main ideas from minor ideas, and essential information from non-essential information.
- Remember that correct answer choices will not be identical to any particular sentence in the passage.

01 Botany

Read the following passage. Then fill in the diagram with the information that you read. `Track 54`

Plant Stems

Stems are the structures that support a plant's buds and leaves, carrying nutrients to all parts of the plant. Water and carbohydrates (sugars) are transported through the stem's interior tissues, which are typically arranged in a concentric ring formation.

The outermost ring, called the phloem, is where carbohydrates are transported from the leaves to the roots. This occurs through a process called the pressure-flow mechanism. A movement called translocation transports nutrients from the source, where carbohydrates are made and stored in the plant, to the sink, where they are needed. Sinks can be roots, flowers, fruits, stems, and young leaves. As carbohydrates enter the phloem from the leaves, water is transported in by osmosis, which causes pressure to build up, pushing the nutrients downward toward the roots.

Conversely, in the innermost ring of the stem, called the xylem, water moves in an upward direction according to the cohesion-tension theory. Since water molecules attract each other (a property called cohesion), more water is pulled up from the plant's root system toward the leaves. This movement causes tension within the stem's xylem, creating continuous, thin columns of water that extend through the stem. As water evaporates within the plant, the tension becomes greater, moving the water molecules up the plant. Additional water from the soil enters through the roots to sustain the process and the life of the plant.

bud:
an undeveloped stem of a plant

concentric:
having a common center

source:
the origin; the place from which something has been obtained

osmosis:
the passing of fluid through a porous membrane

tension:
an opposite force that results from stretching

attract:
to draw toward or pull by physical forces

sustain:
to keep an action or process going

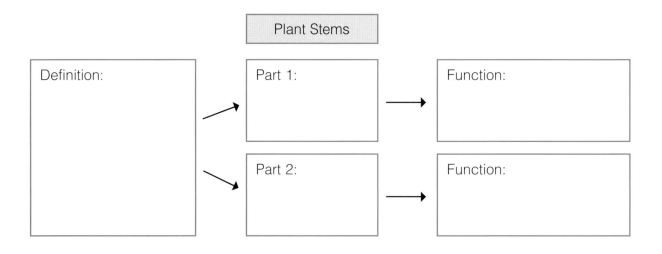

Plant Stems

| Definition: | Part 1: | Function: |
| | Part 2: | Function: |

1. An introductory sentence for a brief summary of the passage is provided below. Complete the summary by selecting the THREE answer choices that express the most important ideas in the passage. Some sentences do not belong in the summary because they express ideas that are not presented in the passage or are minor ideas in the passage. ***This question is worth 2 points.***

Stems are the support structure of a plant's buds and leaves, providing a means of nutrient transport and water replacement.

-
-
-

Answer Choices

(A) The cohesion-tension process within the stem is essential for plant survival.
(B) Nutrients are provided to the plants from the root system.
(C) The xylem of a stem guarantees water delivery to the entire plant.
(D) Carbohydrates are transported through the phloem.
(E) The primary function of a stem is to support the weight of the buds and leaves.
(F) Concentric rings allow for the exchange of water and nutrients.

Fill in the blanks to complete the summary.

Stems are the support structure for a plant's buds and leaves. _____ rings within the stem transport nutrients downward from the _____ to the plant's roots through the pressure-flow mechanism. Water evaporates from the leaves, which _____ more water molecules upward from the roots. This process creates _____ in the interior of the stem for continuous water movement. More water enters through the roots from the soil, _____ the life of the plant.

02 Archaeology

Read the following passage. Then fill in the diagram with the information that you read. `Track 55`

Experimental Archaeology

Experimental archaeology is a subfield of archaeology. It attempts to replicate certain skills of past human cultures. Since excavated artifacts can date back thousands of years, it is important for archaeologists to determine what made them so durable. This information provides essential insight into the lifestyles of past civilizations.

Experimental archaeologists want to understand the relationship between ancient human activities and artifacts left behind. They perform experiments to try to determine how the original articles were created. Their goal is to recreate the entire process using only the primitive materials and methods that would have been available at the time. By studying the artifacts, their approximate age, and the region in which they are found, scientists are able to determine what resources would have been available. They also assess what methods would have been employed in their manufacture using only naturally occurring or handmade implements.

An experiment was conducted to replicate the ancient art of paint making in the southwestern United States. Experimental archaeologists found that minerals, ores, and sedimentary deposits most likely provided the pigments. These rocks were ground into fine, colorful powders with a grinding stone. In order to produce a liquid paint that would adhere to a surface, binding agents were needed. Studies of the paint samples showed that animal fat was the most likely binder used. Fat was extracted from the bone marrow of deer. This was done by an archaeologist experimenting with a hammer stone and granite anvil, tools that the original makers also would have used. The test also proved that the fat and mineral pigments blended together well. However, they were too thick to be applied. Therefore, the roots of yucca, a plant plentiful in the area, were pounded with stones. Then they were soaked with water and squeezed out as a liquid. This substance was combined with the pigment and fat ingredients to create a silky, fluid, durable paint. The entire process replicated the methods and materials most likely used by the ancient paint makers.

replicate: to copy or reproduce
durable: able to last
primitive: the first or earliest of its kind
sedimentary: settling to the bottom
pigment: a material that provides color
extract: to pull something out
anvil: a large block used to shape metals

```
┌─────────────────────────────────┐
│      Experimental Archaeology   │
└─────────────────────────────────┘
```

```
┌──────────────────┐      ┌──────────────────┐      ┌──────────────────┐
│ Definition:      │ ──→  │ Role:            │ ──→  │ Example:         │
│                  │      │                  │      │                  │
│                  │      │                  │      │                  │
│                  │      │                  │      │                  │
└──────────────────┘      └──────────────────┘      └──────────────────┘
```

1. An introductory sentence for a brief summary of the passage is provided below. Complete the summary by selecting the THREE answer choices that express the most important ideas in the passage. Some sentences do not belong in the summary because they express ideas that are not presented in the passage or are minor ideas in the passage. **This question is worth 2 points.**

Experimental archaeology attempts to recreate the methods and materials used to make ancient artifacts.

```
┌─────────────────────────────────────────────────────────────────────────┐
│   •                                                                     │
│                                                                         │
│   •                                                                     │
│                                                                         │
│   •                                                                     │
└─────────────────────────────────────────────────────────────────────────┘
```

Answer Choices

(A) Experimental archaeologists use the actual tools and techniques of ancient peoples.
(B) Ancient paint-making techniques utilized plant, animal, and mineral ingredients.
(C) Animal fat is the principal color-producing agent in most ancient paints.
(D) Experimental archaeologists combine modern techniques with ancient knowledge.
(E) Experimental archaeology attempts to discover how ancient peoples lived.
(F) Studying past human behavior reveals the efficiency of using available materials.

Fill in the blanks to complete the summary.

Experimental archaeology attempts to _____ certain skills of past cultures. By doing this, we can determine what made ancient artifacts so _____. Archaeologists use only the _____ materials and methods available at the time the items were made. One experiment recreated the process of paint-making using ores, minerals, and _____ deposits. Then, animal fat was _____ using tools available at the time. Finally, yucca roots were added to recreate the substance likely made by ancient paint makers.

----

03 History

Read the following passage. Then fill in the diagram with the information that you read. `Track 56`

Entrepreneurs of the California Gold Rush

The gold rush of 1849 in California brought thousands of newcomers to the state. They came in search of fortune and a better life. Although most of them came to dig for gold, other opportunities were inadvertently created for entrepreneurs of a different kind.

The gold rush caused crowded camps to appear all over California, giving rise to competition for basic daily needs. Food, clothing, and other necessities could hardly be produced fast enough to keep up with the growing masses. People from all types of backgrounds quickly discovered that there was just as much fortune to be made serving the gold diggers as there was in digging for gold. With fierce and increasingly violent rivalry to find more gold happening all around them, some people saw an opportunity to make a better living by providing other goods and services to the rapidly growing population. A few had inflated their prices and taken advantage of the miners' plight. However, most were simply honest, hardworking businessmen with creative ideas.

One such entrepreneur was a young merchant named Levi Strauss. He was best known for a prosperous dry goods business that manufactured various types of apparel. Strauss created a pair of sturdy pants out of canvas, which became very popular among the miners. The pants were durable enough to withstand the harsh conditions of the miners' activities: stooping, kneeling, bending, and crawling in mud and on rocky surfaces. Ultimately, he added a critical element to the trousers: the metal rivet, which provided the best reinforcement for the laborers' work wear. This feature, still used in the manufacture of jeans today, changed the course of American fashion and put Mr. Strauss on the road to unparalleled success. Levi Strauss was one of the first of many entrepreneurs to make his fortune during the gold rush without digging for a single nugget.

inadvertently:
unintentionally

entrepreneur:
a risk-taking businessperson

necessity:
something required

rivalry:
a feeling of competition

inflate:
to raise prices

plight:
an unfortunate situation

apparel:
clothing

rivet:
a bolt used to fasten two pieces of material together

reinforcement:
something that strengthens

Entrepreneurship During the California Gold Rush

Cause:

Effect:

Example:

1. An introductory sentence for a brief summary of the passage is provided below. Complete the summary by selecting the THREE answer choices that express the most important ideas in the passage. Some sentences do not belong in the summary because they express ideas that are not presented in the passage or are minor ideas in the passage. *This question is worth 2 points.*

The rapid arrival of people during the California Gold Rush created a pressing need for goods and services.

-
-
-

Answer Choices

(A) The fortune seekers of the gold rush were unable to meet the miners' daily needs.
(B) Miners became hostile over inflating prices of goods and services.
(C) Opportunities arose for new ways in which creative people could earn a living.
(D) Levi Strauss made his fortune by manufacturing durable workmen's trousers.
(E) The rapidly growing population created thriving communities.
(F) The demand for goods and services increased faster than the supply.

Fill in the blanks to complete the summary.

The 1849 gold rush in California _____ created opportunities for entrepreneurs to make their fortunes in ways other than mining. A rapidly growing population increased the demand for basic _____ such as food and clothing. While some merchants _____ their prices to take advantage of the miners' _____, many were honest and hardworking. Levi Strauss was a merchant who sold various types of _____, including a type of work trousers that used metal rivets. This provided a type of pants that fulfilled miners' needs in a new way and led to his success.

----

04 | Astronomy

Read the following passage. Then fill in the diagram with the information that you read. `Track 57`

Why the Sky is Blue

The scattering of sunlight off the molecules in the atmosphere is responsible for the blue appearance of the sky. Usually, we see light in its full visible spectrum, which appears white to the human eye. However, when light rays are broken or refracted by water in the atmosphere, its colors appear separated. This is because each color has its own wavelength.

The reason the sky appears to be blue was first investigated by British physicist Lord Rayleigh. He discovered that sunlight is scattered by water molecules in the air in the same way that white light is scattered by a prism. The visible light spectrum occupies only the portion of the entire electromagnetic radiation field that we can see. The spectrum includes the colors of a rainbow we can sometimes see in the sky. It ranges from red, classified as the longest wavelength, to violet, classified as the shortest. Since this scattering in the sky is more effective at shorter wavelengths where the blue end of the visible spectrum is, the sky appears to be blue. Although all the colors of the visible light spectrum are present in white sunlight, the blue wavelength is most easily detected by the human eye, due to the angle at which we view sunlight.

As we view the sunlight away from the sun, it is scattered through more atmospheric molecules than if we looked more directly toward the sun. This scattering, called Rayleigh scattering, is predominantly in the blue end of the light spectrum. It is because of the shorter wavelength of blue that the light is more effectively scattered. If we look toward the sun, the full spectrum of white light is more dominant; further from the sun, a deeper blue is visible. In other words, the more air molecules light travels through, the more saturation of color we can detect.

scattering:
the process by which things are split apart

spectrum:
the band of colors present in light

refracted:
changed in direction and speed

wavelength:
the distance between two peaks of a wave

range:
to vary within certain limits

predominantly:
mainly; primarily

saturation:
the degree of purity of a color

Why the Sky Is Blue

Theory:

Support 1:

Support 2:

1. An introductory sentence for a brief summary of the passage is provided below. Complete the summary by selecting the THREE answer choices that express the most important ideas in the passage. Some sentences do not belong in the summary because they express ideas that are not presented in the passage or are minor ideas in the passage. **This question is worth 2 points.**

The passage discusses the scientific reasons for the appearance of a blue sky to the human eye.

-
-
-

Answer Choices

(A) The closer we look toward the sun, the more colors of the visible spectrum we can see.
(B) Sunlight scatters off of molecules in the air more effectively at shorter wavelengths.
(C) The sky looks bluer farther from the sun because of the decrease in light waves.
(D) The visible spectrum includes all colors of the rainbow.
(E) Water molecules in the air scatter light in the same way as a prism.
(F) The blue range of colors have short wavelengths.

Fill in the blanks to complete the summary.

The sky appears to be blue because of the _____ of light waves against water molecules in the atmosphere. The colors of the light spectrum we can see _____ from red, which has the longest wavelength, to violet, which has the shortest. When light rays are broken or _____ by water in the atmosphere, colors appear separated because of their wavelengths. The scattering of light molecules in the sky is _____ at the blue end of the light spectrum because of its shorter wavelength, most easily seen by the human eye. Farther from the sun, the greater _____ of color makes the sky appear a deeper blue.

05 | Art History

Read the following passage. Then fill in the diagram with the information that you read. `Track 58`

Stieglitz: Photography as Art

Alfred Stieglitz made art history in the 1920s by advancing his photographic work from simple images of the world captured on film to expressions of artistic interpretation as seen through the lens of his camera.

While spending time in Europe, Stieglitz's photographic skills became widely respected. He returned to New York City in 1890 to become a partner in the Photochrome Engraving Company. The art movement in Europe had been a source of inspiration to him. He soon found himself more interested in promoting photography in the US as an artistic expression than producing standard photographs. His enthusiasm, however, was not as well received in the American art world. The brief but important Dada art movement had gained broad recognition in Europe as a creative social outlet. Stieglitz became involved with the movement in New York. However, it did not have a comparable impact and quickly disbanded. Dada art, however, had a profound impact on the way Stieglitz viewed his work. Consequently, he helped to establish the Camera Club of New York. He also edited and published the periodical *Camera Work*. Both of these endeavors served to promote the artistic side of photography to the public.

Stieglitz focused much of his work on the urban surroundings of New York City. He used the play of shadow and light rather than objects as the main content of his photographs. Stieglitz's series of photographs of clouds and sky was called *Equivalents*. He undertook the project in an effort to demonstrate that form rather than subject was what mattered in creating an expression of visual art. The incorporation of abstract patterns was his way of conveying emotion. By capturing these simple images so completely, Stieglitz believed that all who looked upon it in the future would experience a feeling equivalent to the one he experienced viewing the scene in person. In an unparalleled career that spanned the transition from the Victorian to the modern world of art, Alfred Stieglitz has likely had a more profound influence on the shift toward aesthetic photography than any other individual. His sensibilities toward this evolving art form showed true maturity in his craft. Stieglitz's photography embodied his desire to try new things in order to exhibit beauty in that which previously appeared devoid of it.

expression:
the communication of thoughts and feelings

promote:
to advance

Dada:
an art movement of the early 20th century concerned with strange and nonsensical art

outlet:
a means of expression or satisfaction

impact:
an influence

disband:
to split apart

periodical:
a magazine distributed at regular intervals

equivalent:
similar

aesthetic:
concerned with emotions

Stieglitz Photography

Definition:		Role:		Example:

1. An introductory sentence for a brief summary of the passage is provided below. Complete the summary by selecting the THREE answer choices that express the most important ideas in the passage. Some sentences do not belong in the summary because they express ideas that are not presented in the passage or are minor ideas in the passage. **This question is worth 2 points.**

Alfred Stieglitz attempted to transform photography to an expressionist art form.

- •
- •
- •

Answer Choices

(A) The modern shift of photography was not well accepted in Europe in the 1900s.
(B) Images of clouds and sky were meant to recreate an emotion for the viewer.
(C) Stieglitz was inspired by the non-traditional approach of the Dada art movement.
(D) Stieglitz's partnership in the Photochrome Engraving Company launched his career.
(E) Photography as an art form quickly became popular in the United States.
(F) Stieglitz sought to show beauty in images that were not ordinarily seen as beautiful.

Fill in the blanks to complete the summary.

Alfred Stieglitz was a photographer who made his work a(n) _____ of artistic interpretation of the world around him. Dada art had a profound _____ on the way he viewed photography, so he became interested in the _____ of photography as art. Stieglitz edited and published a photography _____ and focused much of his work on urban surroundings. His *Equivalents* series was intended to completely capture a moment in time, thereby affording the viewer a(n) _____ experience of the feeling of that moment.

06 | Sociology

Read the following passage. Then fill in the diagram with the information that you read. `Track 59`

Socialization and Media

The debate surrounding media's role in socialization intensified after the television was first made commercially available in the 1930s. Today, the role of television is even stronger. According to a leading polling firm, ninety-nine percent of American households own at least one television. The people in those households watch an average of seven hours of television each day. Thus, television is undeniably an important part of modern culture. The benefits of media such as television, however, are debated. Many believe that media provide many social benefits. Others feel that their effect on socialization is entirely negative.

Those in support of media as socializers cite their educational and interactional benefits. Especially for children just learning to socialize, many popular educational programs can help teach valuable life lessons. For example, *Sesame Street*, a popular American television show, focuses on teaching children academic information such as mathematics and valuable social skills like sharing. Various studies have indicated the benefits of this program. One study in particular showed that children who regularly watched *Sesame Street* consistently received higher grades in school than those who did not. Moreover, media can provide people of all ages with topics that allow them to socialize more effectively. For example, television provides a number of popular programs—from news to comedy—that children and adults alike can discuss. A person in a social situation can certainly find a shared topic to discuss from one of the many television programs being broadcast daily.

Those against the media as a socializer find grounds for contention in these same areas. They claim that the education and interaction offered by the media are often negative rather than positive. Programs on television are often not educationally based. This is true even among those designed for children. Many animated children's shows are based on violence. In addition, acts of violence can be witnessed on any local news program. Statistics suggest that the average American will view over 200,000 acts of violence on television by the age of eighteen. These statistics suggest that television teaches violence rather than academics or social skills. Critics of television as a socializer also suggest that, rather than giving people a common ground to discuss topics, it implants often unrealistic stereotypes. These stereotypes can then be perpetuated by those who watch them. For example, a violent television show may be set in a city that, in real life, is very peaceful. However, viewers may develop a bias toward that city due to its representation on the show.

socialization:
the process of learning to socialize with others

intensify:
to become stronger

undeniably:
unquestionably

interactional:
relating to how people converse

grounds:
reason or basis

contention:
an argument; a dispute

implant:
to place into

stereotype:
a simplified or distorted image

The Role of the Media in Socialization

Advantage 1:	Disadvantage 1:
Advantage 2:	Disadvantage 2:

1. An introductory sentence for a brief summary of the passage is provided below. Complete the summary by selecting the THREE answer choices that express the most important ideas in the passage. Some sentences do not belong in the summary because they express ideas that are not presented in the passage or are minor ideas in the passage. **This question is worth 2 points.**

This passage discusses some of the ways in which media act as a socializer.

-
-
-

Answer Choices

(A) Many believe that children should not watch television due to the violence it portrays.
(B) Television viewers often have stereotypes about cities due to negative depictions.
(C) Many television programs benefit children by teaching school subjects and social skills.
(D) Television contains many stereotypes that can be learned and spread by viewers.
(E) Many children's programs contain violence and can teach children the wrong lessons.
(F) While some feel media have a role in socialization, others argue they have no role at all.

Fill in the blanks to complete the summary.

The passage discusses the media's role in socialization, which has only _____

as television's role has grown in society. Television is _____ an important

part of modern culture. The media have educational and _____ advantages

and disadvantages. Many people believe that the media help educate children and give

people common topics to discuss in social settings. However, others believe that the media

promote violence and _____ often unrealistic _____.

Chapter 10 Table/Chart Questions

Necessary Skills

- Recognizing the organization and purpose of a passage
- Understanding rhetorical functions such as cause-effect relationships, compare-contrast relationships, and arguments
- Identifying and organizing important ideas and points from a passage and placing them in the appropriate context

Example Question

- Complete the table below to summarize information about concepts discussed in the passage. Match the appropriate statements to the concepts with which they are associated. TWO of the answer choices will NOT be used. ***This question is worth 3 points.***

Strategies

- Separate main ideas from minor ideas, and essential information from non-essential information.
- Remember that major ideas are ones that would be included in a fairly detailed outline of the passage.

01 Geology

Read the following passage. Then fill in the diagram with the information that you read. `Track 60`

Seismic Waves: P Waves and S Waves

An earthquake generates shock waves traveling out in all directions, both in the Earth's interior and along the Earth's surface. These shock waves are called seismic waves and can be felt by people living many miles away from the earthquake.

P waves and S waves are the two kinds of interior seismic waves. P waves are primary waves that travel outward from where the Earthquake originates beneath the Earth's surface. The fastest of all seismic waves, P waves, can move through any medium of the Earth's interior: solid, liquid, or gas. They alternately compress and expand the medium so that P waves vibrate in the same direction in which they travel.

On the other hand, S waves, or secondary waves, can only travel through solid mediums. They create vibrations at a right angle to the direction in which the waves are traveling. This results in the shaking characteristic of an earthquake, where rocks move up and down or from side to side.

Because the speed of S waves is always slower than that of P waves, scientists can compare the arrival times of the two types of interior waves. This allows them to pinpoint the location of an earthquake, even if it is thousands of miles away.

generate:
to cause

seismic:
relating to vibrations of the Earth

originate:
to begin; to start

medium:
material or surroundings in which something exists or moves through

alternately:
by taking turns; first one and then the other

compress:
to squeeze together

pinpoint:
to identify; to locate

Seismic Waves

Classification 1:
- Attribute 1:
- Attribute 2:
- Attribute 3:

Classification 2:
- Attribute 1:
- Attribute 2:
- Attribute 3:

1. **Directions:** Complete the table below about the types of seismic waves discussed in the passage. Match the appropriate statements to the type of seismic waves with which they are associated. TWO of the answer choices will NOT be used. ***This question is worth 3 points.***

Seismic Wave	Statements
P waves	• • •
S waves	• •

Answer Choices

(A) Travel on the surface of the Earth
(B) Produce vibrations that move in the direction of the waves
(C) Can only move through solids
(D) Produce vibrations that move up and down or side to side
(E) Move through underground water
(F) Are the fastest moving waves
(G) Can vibrate at any angle

Fill in the blanks to complete the summary.

According to the passage, earthquakes _____ shock waves known as seismic waves. Two kinds of seismic waves travel through the Earth's interior. Primary waves, or P waves, travel outward from where an earthquake _____. They can move through solids, liquids, or gases under the surface of the Earth, alternately _____ and expanding them. S waves are secondary waves that can only move through solids. They vibrate at right angles to their direction. S waves travel more slowly than P waves and can only travel through solid _____. Scientists can compare S waves and P waves to _____ the location of earthquakes, even thousands of miles away.

02 | Anthropology

Read the following passage. Then fill in the diagram with the information that you read. `Track 61`

Pastoralists and Hunter-Gatherers

The strategy a non-industrial society uses to obtain the resources its members need to survive—especially food—affects its social organization. Thus, societies using the same system of economic production will share some social characteristics, even though they are located in different parts of the world.

For much of human history, human beings were exclusively hunter-gatherers, foraging to meet their dietary and other needs. In such egalitarian societies, the basic social unit is the band. A band is a group of usually fewer than a hundred people, whose members are related through marriage or kinship. Everyone in the band gets an equal share of meat, and there is great social mobility. People marry outside their own band, so a person can choose to live with bands of his or her parents or grandparents. People can change their band membership several times in a lifetime. After marriage, a woman may move with her husband between her band and his.

About 12,000 years ago, humans developed food production in the form of farming and herding. As societies adopted this new economic strategy, social structures changed. A pastoralist, or herding society, is also based on small groups but is much more hierarchical. The main social unit is the extended family, with a male elder leading his sons and their families. Pastoralists rely on a domesticated herd of animals, for instance, cattle or camels, for food and other products. The herd must be moved from place to place, depending on the seasons, to find food. When the entire group—men, women, and children—move with the herd, anthropologists categorize the movement as "pastoral nomadism." In some herding societies, only part of the group moves with the herd, leaving most of the members behind in a home village. Anthropologists call this "transhumance."

exclusively: only

forage: to look for food

egalitarian: having equal social, political, and economic rights

kinship: a family relationship

adopt: to choose to follow something

hierarchical: separated using different levels of ranking

domesticated: tamed; brought under control for human use

Hunter-Gatherers vs. Pastoralists

Hunter-Gatherers	Both	Pastoralists
•	•	•
•		•
•		•

1. **Directions:** Complete the table below by summarizing the characteristics of hunter-gatherers and pastoralists discussed in the passage. Match the appropriate statements to the society they describe. TWO of the answer choices will NOT be used. *This question is worth 3 points.*

Society	Statements
Hunter-Gatherer	• •
Pastoralist	• • •

Answer Choices

(A) A married woman has a choice of several different groups with whom she can live.
(B) Herds often split into groups that move separately.
(C) Women and elders are the most important members of the group.
(D) About 12,000 years ago, humans thought to develop this method.
(E) Members of the group are treated as equals.
(F) Members own an equal share of herded animals.
(G) Sons usually live in a group with their fathers, even after they marry.

Fill in the blanks to complete the summary.

The way in which a pre-industrial society finds or produces its food affects its social structure. Hunter-gatherer societies, in which members _____ for food, are _____. Members are usually related through marriage or _____. Everyone gets an equal share of the meat, and they can easily move from one band to another. Pastoralist societies are _____. Usually an older male member heads up the group, which consists of his sons and their families. Pastoralists also rely on _____ animals for food and other products.

03 | Philosophy

Read the following passage. Then fill in the diagram with the information that you read. `Track 62`

Plato and Aristotle

Plato and Aristotle were two of the earliest Western political philosophers. While both shared many beliefs—Plato was a teacher of Aristotle—Plato and Aristotle differed on how to achieve a good government.

Plato believed there was a world beyond human senses, a world of what he called Forms. Human senses—sight, hearing, touch, smell, taste—are not perfect and therefore cannot give man a perfect rendering of the world. Instead, it is only through the human mind that man can truly know Forms, that is, reality. In Plato's view, only a small minority of men, genuine philosophers, are capable of obtaining this otherworldly knowledge. For Plato, therefore, the ideal form of government was the philosopher-king. Only a philosopher-king could ensure that the state promotes the ideal of the good life, a concept derived from the world of Forms that only a philosopher could understand. In the absence of a philosopher-king, Plato turned to the rule of law as the subsequent guarantee of good government.

Aristotle defined the problem of governing differently from his teacher, rejecting Plato's theory of Forms. For Aristotle, what is perceived by the senses is indeed the real world, and man can gain knowledge of it through observation and study. Aristotle agreed with Plato that government should promote the good life and the rule of law was necessary to that goal. For Aristotle, however, the rule of law was not a second choice but was preferable to rule by any one man, the concept of a philosopher-king notwithstanding. Aristotle's theory that even the ruler of a state must be subject to its laws formed the underpinning of modern constitutional government.

rendering:
an interpretation

ensure:
to make certain

derive:
to create from an original source

rule of law:
the idea that people are governed by laws that apply to and are known by everyone, and not by orders of rulers

subsequent:
next in a series

underpinning:
a foundation; a support

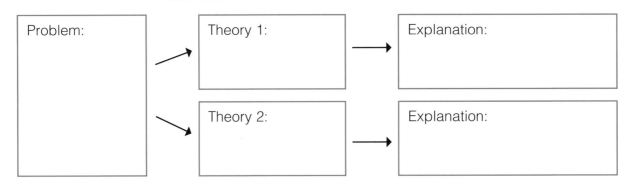

The Philosophies of Plato and Aristotle

Problem:

Theory 1:

Explanation:

Theory 2:

Explanation:

1. **Directions:** Complete the table below to summarize information about the two philosophers discussed in the passage. Match the appropriate statements to the philosopher with which they are associated. TWO of the answer choices will NOT be used. *This question is worth 4 points.*

Philosopher	Statements
Plato	• • • •
Aristotle	• • •

Answer Choices

(A) Man perceives reality through his senses.
(B) Only a philosopher can understand the ideal of the good life.
(C) A world exists that is beyond the human senses.
(D) A constitution is necessary for good government.
(E) The world of Forms is the true reality.
(F) A government based on the rule of law is the best method.
(G) Rule of law is necessary for good government in the absence of a philosopher-king.
(H) A person with well-developed senses can perceive the world of Forms.
(I) Even rulers must follow the laws of the state.

Fill in the blanks to complete the summary.

According to the passage, Plato believed reality existed in a world of Forms that could only be understood by philosophers. Because human senses cannot give a perfect _____ of the world, it is only through the mind that humans can truly know reality. For Plato, the ideal form of government was a philosopher-king, who could _____ that the concept _____ from the world of Forms was promoted. Without a philosopher-king, Plato believed that the rule of law was the _____ form of good government. Aristotle, however, believed that what people perceived through their senses was reality. His theory that even rulers must follow the rule of law formed the _____ of constitutional governments today.

04 | Art History

Read the following passage. Then fill in the diagram with the information that you read. `Track 63`

Baroque/Rococo

The Baroque period in Western architecture spanned the 17th century and first half of the 18th century. The Rococo style then emerged in the early 18th century as a reaction against Baroque excesses. However, it actually was a refinement of Baroque elements.

Four key elements identify Baroque architecture. First, buildings tended to be massive, creating a sense that their importance was larger than life. For example, palaces from the era were visual reminders of the power of the state, and impressive churches encouraged the faithful in their beliefs. Second, painting and sculpture combined with architecture to create a decorative Baroque unity. Sculpture, for instance, was bold and dramatic, like the buildings themselves. Third, to bring that same drama to the interior, Baroque architects used vivid colors and luxurious materials of different textures. One example is the covering of church ceilings with brightly painted scenes. A fourth element was the design and decoration of the interior space. This offered a variety of views leading off the main visual axis of the building, usually leading from the entrance. Here, too, powerful sculpture and lighting effects were used to draw the eye to various parts of the interior. This was done so that the interior offered a series of dramatic and distinct visual experiences.

The Baroque style proved to be too robust for the more graceful tastes of the 18th century. In response, the Rococo style emerged. Rococo, rather than being a style apart from Baroque, is better viewed as a style of decoration applied to Baroque elements. Rococo decoration was more delicate and subtle. By using smaller columns and continuous smooth surfaces in place of contrasting textures, Rococo buildings appeared less massive and imposing. While the integration of painting and sculpture with architecture remained important in Rococo design, Rococo sculptors preferred to work on a smaller, more intimate scale. Pastel tones replaced the vivid colors of the Baroque style, and mirrors were popular decorations. Graceful S-and C-shaped swirls and curves decorated walls and ceilings so much that critics attacked the style for its overuse of ornamental decorations. Windows were added to building designs to let in more light. This either softened the impression of the interior or created a dramatic effect. In general, though, interior space became more unified, rather than drawing the eye to various dramatic views.

refinement:
a slight change; a small improvement

axis:
an imaginary straight line through the center of something

robust:
forceful; strong; tough

subtle:
not very obvious; suggestive

imposing:
overwhelming; impressive

integration:
the state of combination; a mixing together to make a whole

	Baroque vs. Rococo	

Baroque	Both	Rococo
• • •	•	• • •

1. **Directions:** Complete the table below with information about the two styles of architecture discussed in the passage. Match the appropriate statements to the style of architecture they describe. TWO of the answer choices will NOT be used. ***This question is worth 3 points.***

Architectural Style	Statements
Baroque	• • •
Rococo	• •

Answer Choices

(A) Swirls and curves were used in interior design.
(B) Sculptures tended to be smaller and less dramatic.
(C) Palaces were especially massive and imposing.
(D) Painting did not contribute to the overall style.
(E) Different, dramatic views were used in the design of the interior.
(F) Style emphasized simplicity and plain designs.
(G) Paintings using bright colors decorated church interiors.

Fill in the blanks to complete the summary.

There are four key elements of Baroque architecture. Buildings were massive.
Architecture, painting, and sculpture worked together. The interiors used bright colors and
different materials, and there were dramatic views off the main visual _____.
Baroque architecture was too _____ for the tastes of the time. However, Rococo
architecture was a(n) _____ of these elements. Its decoration was more
delicate and _____. It also featured the _____ of painting and
sculpture with its architecture.

----

05 | Sociology

Read the following passage. Then fill in the diagram with the information that you read. `Track 64`

The Idea of Race

Centuries of conventional wisdom held that human beings could be divided into races that have a basis in the science of biology. Yet early usage of the word "race" did not assume any biological foundation. As its definition changed over time, however, it eventually claimed a scientific foundation.

When the word "race" first entered the English language, it had a meaning quite different from its more current association. Race simply denoted a group of people who shared an identity. "The human race" included all human beings. The term could also identify people who shared a national interest, as in "the Czech race," or "the Brazilian race." It also referred to a way of life, such as "a race of hunter-gatherers."

Explorations in the 16th and 17th centuries affected the definition of race. These journeys brought Europeans into contact with cultures quite different from their own. The people they encountered were also noticeably different in physical characteristics. It was during this time of European conquest and colonization that racial categories became defined by physical appearance. At the same time, science was evolving, and attempts were made to measure "racial differences."

As people were racially categorized by their physical attributes such as skin color, head shape, and hair texture, another important idea associated with race developed. A "racial worldview" assumed that each race had its own behavioral and physical traits that were passed on from parents to children. These traits could therefore be used to distinguish each race. Three commonly used categories were Caucasoid, Mongoloid, and Negroid. A mid-19th century treatise, "Essay on the Inequality of Human Races," lent further support to the idea that race was a biological explanation for human differences that could thus be legitimately used to rank human beings.

As the 20th century dawned, the idea behind the concept of race—that humans could be readily divided into biologically determined races—was widely accepted. However, scientists found it increasingly difficult to actually measure those biological determinants. As genetic studies in the late 20th century were to confirm, the reason was simple. Races have no biological foundation. There is no "race" gene. It turns out that so-called races are neither based on biology nor definable in a scientific manner. Today, sociologists and other scientists recognize that "race" is a cultural construct. It identifies a group that shares some visible physical traits, as well as some cultural and historical experiences.

conventional:
following generally accepted beliefs

association:
a connection of ideas

denote:
to mean; to refer to

distinguish:
to tell apart from something

treatise:
a formal, written work addressing a subject extensively

rank:
to assign a certain position or place, for instance, a social class

construct:
an idea or perception based on impressions from the senses

```
┌─────────────────────────────────────┐
│      The Changing Ideas of Race      │
└─────────────────────────────────────┘
```

Meaning 1:	Meaning 2:	Meaning 3:

1. **Directions:** Complete the table below to summarize information about the concepts of race discussed in the passage. Match the appropriate statements to the era with which they are associated. TWO of the answer choices will NOT be used. **This question is worth 3 points.**

Period	Concept of Race
Original Usage	•
16th and 17th Centuries	• •
20th Century	• •

Answer Choices

(A) Divided people into races according to physical traits
(B) Used definitions for race acquired from foreign countries during the European colonization
(C) Stated that parents pass racial characteristics to their children
(D) Said that a race of people shared a lifestyle
(E) Proved that races are not determined by biology
(F) Described race as a cultural creation
(G) Changed the definition of race in reaction to a 19th-century essay

Fill in the blanks to complete the summary.

   According to the passage, it was _____ wisdom that race simply

_____ a group of people who shared an identity, such as being from the same

country. Race meant something much different from its current _____. Later,

people thought race was a biological fact. It was believed that certain physical and behavioral

traits could be used to _____ each race. Finally, scientists showed there was

no scientific basis for the idea of race, and it was actually a cultural _____.

----

06 | Economics

Read the following passage. Then fill in the diagram with the information that you read. `Track 65`

Keynes and Friedman

Until the 1930s, governments trying to improve a country's economy followed the "quantity theory of money." It argues that the supply of money has an effect upon the strength of the economy. In the 20th century, two Western economists revisited the quantity theory to develop new yet conflicting theories on how government actions can influence the economy.

In 1936, John Maynard Keynes criticized the quantity theory in his *General Theory of Employment, Interest, and Money*. He argued that the money supply did not have a significant effect on prices or the strength of the economy. Keynes believed that the key to a healthy economy was the demand for goods and services produced. His theory is known as a "demand-side" theory. If there is not enough demand for the goods and services companies produce, the companies will produce less. This means that they will employ fewer people. For Keynes, three variables affect demand: consumer spending, government spending, and investment spending. Therefore, to improve the economy, a government can alter its tax and budget policies and encourage investment. For instance, if consumers pay fewer taxes, they are likely to spend more on goods and services, thereby increasing demand. Keynes's work formed the basis of a new branch of economics called Keynesian economics. It became so widely accepted that for several decades, economists rejected monetary policy as a way of managing the volume of economic activity.

In the 1960s, Milton Friedman introduced his "supply-side" economic theories. It brought focus back to the supply of money in an economy. Friedman argued that the money supply has a causal effect on the economy. For him, the fiscal disaster of the Great Depression was not a result of low demand as suggested by Keynes. Rather, it was a contraction in the money supply. The Federal Reserve, the centralized banking system in the US, supplied less money than was desired. This caused a drop in consumption and thus a decline in the overall health of the market. A detailed analysis published by Friedman and a colleague, A *Monetary History of the United States, 1867-1960*, persuaded many that his theories were valid. According to this monetarism school of thought, a steady rate of economic growth can be promoted by a steady growth of the money supply. Simply put, more available money for spending will increase production and employment. Friedman argued against the Keynesian focus on government fiscal policy. He and his fellow monetarists believed that the government should only intervene in the economy by controlling the rate of growth of the money supply.

revisit:
to consider again

variable:
something that changes or can change

monetary:
of or about money

causal:
being a cause of something

fiscal:
financial; having to do with government policies of spending and taxing

contraction:
a reduction in size; a shrinking

consumption:
the purchase or use of goods and services

intervene:
to enter or come between in order to affect something

Keynes vs. Friedman

Keynes	Both	Friedman
• • •	•	• • •

1. **Directions:** Complete the table below to summarize information about the economic theories discussed in the passage. Match the appropriate statements to the theory with which they are associated. TWO of the answer choices will NOT be used. *This question is worth 3 points.*

Theory	Statements
Keynesian	• • •
Monetarist	• •

Answer Choices

(A) Governments need to control the supply of money in order to affect the economy.
(B) Governments should not try to influence the economy.
(C) Governments can change tax policies to change consumer spending.
(D) The employment rate will fall without sufficient demand.
(E) The health of an economy depends on three kinds of spending.
(F) The economy will be negatively affected by a contracted supply of money.
(G) Increases in the tax rate will promote a healthy economy.

Fill in the blanks to complete the summary.

Two economists developed new theories on how governments can influence the economy. Keynesian economists believe that three _____ affect economic activity: consumer spending, government spending, and investment. Keynes's theories became so widely accepted that economists rejected _____ policy to manage economic activity. On the other hand, Friedman's monetarists believe that money supplies have a(n) _____ effect on the economy. They attribute the _____ disaster of the Great Depression to a(n) _____ in the money supply, causing the market to decline.

Vocabulary Review 3

Instructions: Choose the best word or phrase to complete each sentence.

1. During the winter, animals such as deer and fire ants _____ for food that will feed them through the cold months.
   - (A) distinguish
   - (B) forage
   - (C) discern
   - (D) foster

2. The new health club downtown caters _____ to women and their needs.
   - (A) sedimentary
   - (B) randomly
   - (C) inevitably
   - (D) exclusively

3. Astronomers were surprised when they finally pinpointed the _____ of the intense microwaves from space.
   - (A) source
   - (B) reinforcement
   - (C) spectrum
   - (D) kinship

4. Glazes used on materials such as stoneware and porcelain make pottery very strong and _____.
   - (A) profitable
   - (B) durable
   - (C) recreational
   - (D) variable

5. The employee's open defiance of company policy was _____ for dismissal, so she was fired immediately.
   - (A) treatise
   - (B) proximity
   - (C) grounds
   - (D) subject

6. Scientists believe that leprosy, a disease widely thought to have spread from India, in fact appears to have _____ in Africa or the Near East.
   - (A) originated
   - (B) cultivated
   - (C) envisioned
   - (D) replicated

7. The long-standing _____ between the two baseball teams made their games more exciting for their devoted fans.
   - (A) dissipation
   - (B) deluge
   - (C) contention
   - (D) rivalry

8. The Czech Republic has the highest annual per capita _____ of beer in the world.
   - (A) expression
   - (B) rationale
   - (C) consumption
   - (D) territory

Instructions: Choose the word or phrase closest in meaning to the underlined part of each sentence.

9. The local department store sold all types of <u>clothing</u>: work, casual, and dress.
   - (A) apparel
   - (B) tension
   - (C) bondage
   - (D) hardship

10. It is possible for some lizards to <u>grow</u> new tails after losing their tails.
    - (A) sustain
    - (B) generate
    - (C) promote
    - (D) ensure

11. Because the sisters fought constantly over which television show to watch, their mother finally had to <u>mediate</u> and choose one for them.

(A) adopt
(B) intervene
(C) thrive
(D) indulge

12. Because of its large surface area, temperatures in parts of Canada can <u>vary</u> from forty degrees below zero to thirty-five degrees above zero.

(A) implant
(B) shape
(C) execute
(D) range

13. Mahayana Buddhism is the <u>main</u> religion in China, Japan, Korea, and much of Vietnam.

(A) commercial
(B) subsequent
(C) predominant
(D) inherent

14. Phil <u>unintentionally</u> told his aunt about her surprise birthday party because no one had told him that it was a secret.

(A) formally
(B) undeniably
(C) considerably
(D) inadvertently

15. Many scientists believe that the descendants of wolves, jackals, or coyotes were interbred and evolved into <u>tamed</u> companions for humans.

(A) domesticated
(B) conventional
(C) tranquil
(D) fundamental

Instructions: Write the missing words. Use the words below to fill in the blanks.

stereotypes	denotes	underpinning
ranking		construct

The term caste **16.** _____ one's rank or position in society according to birth, occupation, or some other criterion. Many nations face issues of social inequality. Perhaps nowhere else in the world is it such an elaborate **17.** _____ as the Indian institution of caste. Caste has long been an **18.** _____ of Indian culture, but in recent years it has been severely criticized by both Indian and foreign observers. Although some claim that caste has been abolished, such statements do not reflect reality. Caste has undergone significant changes, but it still involves **19.** _____ and discrimination against hundreds of millions of people. India's constitution forbids negative public discrimination on the basis of caste. However, caste **20.** _____ has occurred for centuries and will likely continue.

Instructions: Match the words that are similar in meaning.

21. extract   (A) strong
22. imposing   (B) take out
23. robust   (C) overwhelming
24. primitive   (D) requirement
25. necessity   (E) simple

Mini Test 3

01 Health

Read the passage and answer the questions. `Track 66`

Tinnitus

Hearing is a complex process involving bones, cells, and blood vessels. When these do not work correctly, some people may experience distracting humming, buzzing, ringing, or whistling sounds inside their heads. This perception of sounds, known as tinnitus, has frustrating complications.

Not a disease itself, tinnitus is a symptom caused by various conditions. These may include injury due to loud noises or foreign objects, or ear infections. Millions of people experience tinnitus on some level, and by treating the underlying problem, it can disappear in a short period of time. Those suffering from it experience a ringing noise that is usually not an actual sound. The noise may be in one or both ears and varies in pitch and volume. In some cases, the sound is so loud it disrupts concentration or hampers proper hearing. People can suffer from two types of tinnitus: objective or subjective.

Objective tinnitus is unique because, unlike most cases of tinnitus, patients suffering from it may have an audible sound emanating from their ears that a clinician can actually detect. This arises from muscle spasms around the middle ear, which can emit a clicking or cracking reverberation. Some experience a rhythmic throbbing, repeating in time to a pulse. Pulsatile tinnitus, usually objective in nature, is caused by altered blood flow or increased blood turbulence in proximity to the ear, resulting in the audible sound of blood moving through the veins. Objective tinnitus is very uncommon; most people suffer from subjective tinnitus.

Although there are many causes of subjective tinnitus, the most typical are conditions that can cause hearing loss, such as exposure to excessively loud noises or natural aging. These may have lasting effects or may only cause brief hearing problems. Other causes of subjective tinnitus can include lead poisoning, chemotherapy, and Lyme disease. The mechanisms of subjective tinnitus vary. Microscopic hairs located on the end of auditory cells in the ears can be bent or broken, thus misreading sound or sending signals to the brain of sound that is nonexistent. Direct trauma to the ear can also create the ringing sound, but other causes are relatively unknown.

Researchers recently introduced two categories of subjective tinnitus. Symptoms caused by disorders of the inner ear or acoustic nerve are <u>otic</u>. Somatic symptoms are caused by nerves within the head and brain but outside of the ear. Although there are no specific cures for tinnitus, therapy and adequate rest often help the symptoms recede over time.

▶ **otic** *of, relating to, or located near the ear*

1. **Directions:** An introductory sentence for a brief summary of the passage is provided below. Complete the summary by selecting the THREE answer choices that express the most important ideas in the passage. Some sentences do not belong in the summary because they express ideas that are not presented in the passage or are minor ideas in the passage. *This question is worth 2 points.*

    The condition known as tinnitus causes ringing in the ears and is a symptom of other medical conditions.

    -
    -
    -

    Answer Choices

    (A) Blood flow interference can cause pulsatile tinnitus.
    (B) Buzzing within the ear indicates that tinnitus is present.
    (C) An audible sound coming from the ear characterizes objective tinnitus.
    (D) Antibiotics are helpful in treating medical conditions, whether natural or injury-related.
    (E) Subjective tinnitus has many causes but few explanations for the resulting symptoms.
    (F) Symptoms within the ear are worse than those from outside sources.

02 Business

Read the passage and answer the questions. `Track 67`

Coupons

To sell manufactured products, companies must establish a need or an incentive that persuades consumers to buy. Many businesses have provided an appealing answer to the challenge. By offering coupons that provide a discount on specific goods, consumers feel better about their spending and companies still receive a profit.

Couponing is not a new concept. C.W. Post Co. first introduced coupons in 1895 when it offered penny-off coupons to increase sales of its breakfast cereal. Such cents-off coupons remain the oldest, most widely used, and most effective sales promotion tools available to suppliers. Manufacturers have used all varieties of coupons, from direct mail to instant coupons to newspaper inserts, the most common couponing choice. Stores have increased couponing in the past several decades, and subsequently, shoppers are responding. In the US, over eighty percent of consumers use coupons, and nearly twenty-five percent claim to use them every time they shop.

Many advantages exist in the production and use of coupons. Each coupon serves a dual purpose. While offering the customer a price break, it also increases profits and brand recognition for the manufacturer. Popular with new as well as established companies, coupons make it possible to offer a price reduction only to price-sensitive consumers, without lowering the overall price of the product. Additionally, consumers are more likely to try a new product with a discount coupon because the perceived spending is less. When experiencing a decline in sales, established companies can issue coupons to encourage past buyers to purchase again and entice new users to try the product.

Disadvantages of coupons do occur for the companies involved. To print and distribute coupons, businesses undertake certain costs. Usually, sellers print an expiration date on their coupons. However, they intend for consumers to purchase the product as soon as the coupons are issued rather than at the end of the specified time frame. Until consumers choose to buy, the company's incurred costs are not offset by their purchases. Thus, the consumers dictate when the companies receive their profits. Additionally, companies whose intention was to increase sales may not notice an increase for several months. Much responsibility lies with the consumer. Consumer response to a coupon usually takes between two and six months, and coupons are most frequently redeemed just prior to the expiration date that is stated on the coupon.

▸ **direct mail** *advertising sent directly to prospective customers via the mail*
▸ **brand recognition** *a customer's awareness of a particular brand*

1. **Directions:** An introductory sentence for a brief summary of the passage is provided below. Complete the summary by selecting the THREE answer choices that express the most important ideas in the passage. Some sentences do not belong in the summary because they express ideas that are not presented in the passage or are minor ideas in the passage. *This question is worth 2 points.*

Couponing is an effective sales tool used by companies to increase profits by offering the consumer incentives to purchase their product.

-

-

-

Answer Choices

(A) Manufacturing coupons costs the company and reduces profits.
(B) Couponing has increased significantly over the past few decades.
(C) Expiration dates and coupon use affect company profits.
(D) C.W. Post Co. initiated the use of coupons as a successful promotional tool.
(E) Companies offer coupons in order to advertise and raise buyer interest.
(F) Customers who use coupons are more conscious of price.

03 Biology

Read the passage and answer the questions.   `Track 68`

Virions and Prions

Infections are caused by microorganisms that invade the cells of the body. They cause damage to the tissue and interfere with normal cell activity. Two types of infectious particles, virions and prions, cause multiple health problems. These can range from minor to fatal. While both infectious agents cause disease, their inherent structure and behavior are different, so the effects on the human body are diverse.

A virion is the infectious form of a complete virus particle. It consists of genetic material and a protective protein shell called a capsid. Virions are not capable of reproducing alone, so they infect a host cell in order to replicate themselves. On the other hand, a proteinaceous infectious particle, commonly referred to as a prion, is a microorganism composed solely of protein that causes serious infection. These diseases affect the structure of the brain and other neural tissue. They can disrupt normal nerve communication within the brain.

Regarding its structure, a virion is essentially a gene transporter existing in its simplest form as nucleic acid. It is surrounded by a protective capsid that serves as the shape of the organism. Conversely, prions are made up of proteins found in the human body that have an altered structure. They are resistant to the enzymes that normally break down protein. Scientists believe that prions infect the body by refolding abnormally and converting normal protein molecules into an irregular structure.

Human diseases caused by viruses include influenza and chicken pox, as well as more serious infections such as AIDS and Ebola. Because virions inhabit a host cell, researchers find it difficult to eradicate the infection without killing healthy human cells. Vaccinations prove to be the most effective preventative for infection. Medications exist that treat symptoms of a viral infection, although the virus itself cannot be destroyed. Whereas researchers have found ways to prevent virions from infecting the body, prions are resistant to all medication and procedures. They cause neurodegenerative diseases, which are evident by such symptoms as convulsions (violent, uncontrollable body movements), dementia (an illness that gradually destroys brain function), and personality changes. These ominous diseases that degenerate the body include mad-cow disease and other forms of Creutzfeldt-Jakob disease. The incubation period in which a prion-induced disease develops is slow. However, it progresses rapidly once symptoms appear, causing brain damage that leads to death. Thus, there is no effective treatment for diseases caused by prions.

▸ **nucleic acid** *an acid such as DNA or RNA that is found in the cells of all living things*
▸ **neurodegenerative disease** *condition in which cells in the brain or spinal cord are lost*

1. **Directions:** Complete the table below to summarize information about the infectious agents discussed in the passage. Match the appropriate agents to the characteristics with which they are associated. TWO of the answer choices will NOT be used. ***This question is worth 3 points.***

Infectious Agents	Characteristics
Virions	• •
Prions	• • •

Answer Choices

(A) Can be prevented before infection
(B) Have effects that last a limited amount of time
(C) Cause irreversible damage to tissues
(D) Are composed of matter found in the body
(E) Can be eliminated effectively with medication
(F) Form an abnormal and irregular structure
(G) Include a piece of genetic material that is replicated

04 History

Read the passage and answer the questions.   `Track 69`

The Disappearance of Dinosaurs

The prehistoric dinosaurs that roamed the Earth millennia ago vanished from history without leaving clear indications of what transpired. It was widely believed that dinosaurs and other prehistoric species met their end as a result of the meteor that formed today's Chicxulub crater. The meteor shook the Earth millions of years ago when it landed on the Yucatan Peninsula. It may have been a piece of a much larger asteroid that broke apart in distant space. The theory explains that when the meteor crashed into Mexico, leaving a 112-mile-wide depression and worldwide destruction in its wake, it caused the extinction of the dinosaurs.

However, growing evidence supports a new theory. It states that the extinction that took place at the end of the Cretaceous Period approximately sixty-five million years ago was caused by a series of events. These include the impacts of multiple meteors, heavy volcanic activity in India, and climate changes. Paleontologist Gerta Keller, supported by the National Science Foundation, has been building evidence to prove the new theory according to scientific findings.

Keller gathered information proving that the Chicxulub impact could not have caused the mass extinction. It appears to have predated the extinction by 300,000 years. Paleontologists extracted samples of marine microfossils from sediment layers above and below the Chicxulub impact layer. No significant biotic changes were found in the samples.

Given the magnitude and number of species that became extinct, Keller's theory more likely explains what truly happened. The Chicxulub crater undoubtedly had an effect on the Earth and its inhabitants. However, it would not have been enough to cause a mass extinction, wiping out thousands of species in a relatively short time. Fossils show that many species lived beyond the meteor's impact. Keller describes other factors that played a part. For example, constant volcanic activity released greenhouse gases, which caused a warming effect, produced acid rain, and raised the temperature of the ocean. At this time, marine species evolved to survive in the changed atmosphere. Neither Chicxulub nor volcanoes caused extinction, but they placed great stress on most species. It was the impact of a larger meteor that was the final factor.

All these events weakened Earth's inhabitants and culminated in an impact of colossal proportions. By the time the larger meteor hit, the creatures could not withstand the changes. Although it is not confirmed, some believe the large meteor landed in India, leaving a crater an estimated 300 miles wide. The meteor and resulting crater had to be of great significance given the resulting destruction.

▶ **biotic** *pertaining to life or living*
▶ **colossal** *of great size or extent*

1. **Directions:** Complete the table below to summarize information about the two theories behind the extinction of the dinosaurs discussed in the passage. Match the appropriate statements to the theory with which they are associated. TWO of the answer choices will NOT be used. ***This question is worth 4 points.***

Theory	Statements
Chicxulub Theory	• • •
Keller's Theory	• • • •

Answer Choices

(A) Multiple volcanic eruptions caused dinosaurs to die.
(B) A piece of a large asteroid may have broken away in space and hit Earth.
(C) An object from outer space left a crater on the Yucatan Peninsula.
(D) Global warming caused by volcanic activity contributed to extinction.
(E) Dinosaurs became extinct because of a meteor's impact on Earth.
(F) Volcanic eruptions released toxic gases and caused acid rain.
(G) The end of the Cretaceous Period showed an increase in dinosaur species.
(H) Dinosaur species weakened after years of stressful living conditions.
(I) The Earth was bombarded by multiple meteors that diminished dinosaur numbers.

Practice Test

Track 70

Section	Options		Time		Directions	Tools			
Reading	Pause	Section Exit	00 : 20 : 00	Hide	Continue	Volume	Confirm	Next	Help

Reading Section

Directions

In this section, you will read five passages and then answer reading comprehension questions about each passage. Most questions are worth one point, but the last question in each set is worth more than one point. The directions indicate how many points you may receive.

You will have 100 minutes to read all of the passages and answer the questions. Some passages include a word or phrase that is <u>underlined in blue</u>. For those words, you will see a definition or an explanation below the passage.

You can skip questions and go back to them later as long as there is time remaining.

When you are ready to continue, press **Continue** to go to the next page.

01 Psychology

Moral Behavior

The dictionary defines morality as "being in accord with standards of right or good conduct." The argument over whether our moral behavior is innate or whether it is developed by our environment and culture has been raging for ages. Many people feel morality is based on reason, while others feel it comes from religion or one's own spirituality. Biologists believe that humans' tendency to obey the Golden Rule—"Do unto others as you would have them do unto you"—is a product of evolution.

■ **A)** At first, moral behavior seems to oppose the rules of Charles Darwin's theory of survival of the fittest and natural selection. ■ **B)** However, researchers in the field of biology feel that as animals evolved to live in groups, the propensity to look only after one's own needs had to fade in order for a group mentality to emerge. ■ **C)** To ensure the group's success as a whole, every member had to look out for the interests of the majority, a concept known as utilitarianism. ■ **D)** This is a system of beliefs based on what does the greatest good for the greatest number of people.

A researcher named Jonathan Haidt at the University of Virginia believes that morality is driven by two separate mindsets—one ancient and one modern. Dr. Haidt declares that the human mind is unaware of the distinction between the two. The ancient mental system is based on the emotion behind moral behaviors, which is a type of intuitive sense of what is right and wrong that evolved before language developed. These are the "gut reactions" people experience in tough situations that call for quick action. The more modern system of thought came with the development of language, as people became able to express verbally why something was right or wrong. The two work together when we are put in morally compromising situations. When confronted with a moral dilemma, one's intuition immediately decides what is right or wrong. Rational thought and judgment about the morality of an issue follow the decision that one's emotional reaction already made.

Dr. Haidt identified five areas of moral conduct that are common in most countries and systems throughout the world, and he describes these as the foundation for all moral behavior. These moral components conceptualize how people treat others and what is important in being part of a group. Regardless of their background, religion, socioeconomic status, or educational level, Dr. Haidt found that the majority of people hold to these moral concepts. The first moral concept is the prevention of harm. Generally, people believe that it is wrong to harm another human being or animal for cruel and needless reasons. The second moral concept is fairness, which holds that all people should be treated fairly. For instance, people should treat the poor in the same manner as the wealthy, and the weak the same as the strong. The third moral concept is loyalty to one's group. This entails a strong devotion to the values of the group as a whole. People with strong loyalties believe that adherence to the laws of society is important because it upholds the integrity of that society. The idea of loyalty is closely interwoven with the fourth moral foundation: respect for authority. People who value authority believe in the strength of a governing body and a strong hierarchy with established roles and rules. The fifth concept involves upholding high standards of purity. This deals with the way that members of a group view their bodies. The idea of purity comes into play in the standards of cleanliness in society. Daily hygiene routines, eating food that has not been contaminated in some way, and burial rules and rituals fall into this category.

Dr. Haidt's research concludes that these moral concepts are inherent in our physical makeup and are learned behaviors, reinforced by our environments from a very early age. The five moral foundations are interpreted differently from society to society, and people rate them differently in order of importance. While morality may take different forms across the many different cultures of the world, it remains true that the basic task of morality, restraining selfishness, is a part of all humanity's moral behavior.

▶ **intuitive**
   knowing or perceiving things instinctively

▶ **moral dilemma**
   a situation in which one has to choose between right and wrong

▶ **socioeconomic status**
   determined by one's education, occupation, lifestyle, and income

1. The word innate in the passage is closest in meaning to
   (A) expected
   (B) instinctive
   (C) sincere
   (D) predictable

2. Why does the author mention the Golden Rule in paragraph 1?
   (A) To contrast moral behavior with immoral behavior
   (B) To prove that people generally know right from wrong
   (C) To suggest that evolution shaped morality
   (D) To define the idea of moral behavior

3. Look at the four squares [■] that indicate where the following sentence could be added to the passage.

   In other words, evolution appears to favor individuals who have learned how to get what they need in order to survive.

   Where would the sentence best fit?
   (A) First square
   (B) Second square
   (C) Third square
   (D) Fourth square

4. According to the passage, morality developed because
   (A) people learned to communicate using spoken language
   (B) people had to learn to survive in groups
   (C) people were born with the ability to know right and wrong
   (D) people learned moral behavior from their ancestors

5. The word propensity in the passage can best be defined as
   (A) sincerity
   (B) weakness
   (C) tendency
   (D) helplessness

6. Which of the following best expresses the essential information in the highlighted sentence? Incorrect answer choices change the meaning in important ways or leave out essential information.
   (A) The earlier mindset based morality on an inborn, emotional understanding of what is proper and acceptable.
   (B) Old-fashioned ways of thinking based goodness on the way a person felt about a situation.
   (C) Theories about ancient attitudes claimed language was not necessary to determine moral behavior.
   (D) Emotions governed the morality of people in ancient times before they developed a way to communicate.

7. Which of the following is NOT correct about the five moral concepts?
   (A) They typically develop in sequential order.
   (B) They serve as the core of all moral behaviors.
   (C) They vary in importance from country to country.
   (D) They explain the various ideas that drive moral behavior.

8. Which of the following can be inferred about Dr. Haidt's five areas of moral conduct?

(A) They are disputed in various cultures.
(B) Aspects of them appear in the laws of many countries.
(C) Many leaders would likely disagree with their loyalty principles.
(D) They are based on innate human tendencies.

9. What can be inferred about humanity as a whole based on Dr. Haidt's moral concepts?

(A) Morality is a universal characteristic that applies to the whole world.
(B) The natural world plays a major role in the development of morality.
(C) Morality is an instinctive characteristic that humans have from birth.
(D) People from different cultures will not value the same principles.

10. According to the passage, morality

(A) conflicts with Darwin's theory of natural selection
(B) goes against the dominant authority
(C) seeks to restrict human selfishness
(D) includes generosity as an important moral

11. The word entails in the passage is closest in meaning to
(A) follows
(B) produces
(C) causes
(D) involves

12. The word This in paragraph 4 refers to
(A) A strong hierarchy
(B) The fifth concept
(C) A governing body
(D) Upholding high standards

13. **Directions:** An introductory sentence for a brief summary of the passage is provided below. Complete the summary by selecting the THREE answer choices that express the most important ideas in the passage. Some answer choices do not belong in the summary because they express ideas that are not presented in the passage or are minor ideas in the passage. ***This question is worth 2 points.***

Moral behavior has certain characteristics that are common to most countries throughout the world.

-
-
-

Answer Choices

(A) Utilitarianism is a belief based on what does the greatest good for the greatest number of people.
(B) Morality is an outcome of evolution that made living in groups possible for humans.
(C) Many people believe that morality is based mostly on reason.
(D) Dr. Haidt has identified five moral principles that most countries share: freedom from harm, fairness, loyalty, respect for authority, and purity.
(E) Those who value loyalty believe that rules should be followed regardless.
(F) Morality is a combination of innate qualities and learned behaviors.
(G) Freedom from harm is the belief that no creature should be hurt needlessly.

02 History

Ancient Angkor

In the regions of Southeast Asia dwell the remains of an era that far exceeded its time in developments and industrialization. This ancient city, which was mysteriously deserted in the 15th century, is known as Angkor. Located in Cambodia, Angkor was established in 802 CE as the seat of the Khmer Empire. Khmer was the largest continuous empire in Southeast Asia. Its main city of Angkor grew and developed until it was abandoned in the year 1431. Many historians theorize as to why it was abandoned, but the mystery remains.

Angkor was a city of power, industry, architecture, and cultural unity, which is why speculation surrounds its decline. The ancient Khmer city stretched over an area of nearly 120 square miles, comparable to present-day Los Angeles. Each successive ruler to the throne brought significant additions that diversified the territory. One ruler is known for constructing a baray, a massive water reservoir. Another built the imposing Angkor Wat, a temple of great proportions that survived the city's demise and exists today as a Buddhist temple. Along with over seventy other temples in the region, Angkor was home to an expansive waterworks of marked ingenuity when nothing of its kind existed in the world. The civilization was structured around the Mekong River. Intricate and sophisticated irrigation systems were fashioned to transport water to people and fields in all parts of the city, including those removed from the central water source. For this, the city became known as the "Hydraulic City." The people of Angkor were led by an extensive court system, made up of religious and secular nobles as well as artisans, fishermen, rice farmers, soldiers, and elephant keepers. The civilization was guarded by an army transported by elephants and ruled by shrewd and powerful kings. Yet after 600 years of existence, an abandoned shell was all that remained.

The land, buildings, and architecture were reclaimed by the surrounding forest regions until the 19th century, when French archaeologists discovered the remains and began restoring sites in the great city of Angkor. Since then, theories have evolved over time relating to the death of Angkor's civilization. The first theory states that the city fell because of war. The last two centuries of Angkor's existence showed a decline in the Khmer Empire's population and power. Ongoing wars with neighboring Thailand had devastated the nation. In 1431, attackers from Thai nations invaded and looted Angkor, leaving it desolate and vacant. Continuous war with Thailand culminating in a final attack on the city could have weakened the empire and led to the city's demise.

Another theory states that a change in religion led to the country's downfall. The Khmer

Empire had predominately been a Hindu nation, and the people were unified in their religion. Jayavarman VII, acclaimed as the greatest of Angkor's kings, took the throne in 1181 CE. He instituted a change in religion from Hinduism to Mahayana Buddhism. This action subsequently could have destroyed the unity of the people and the overall foundation of the empire.

■ **A)** Natural disaster is another feasible possibility for the scattering of people from the Angkor region. ■ **B)** Historians say earthquakes, floods, and drastic climate changes would have been capable of stripping Angkor of its people. ■ **C)** One researcher hypothesized that the city suffered from a lack of water due to the transition from the medieval warm period to the little ice age. Others dismiss this idea. ■ **D)**

However, a recently developed theory built on the work of French archaeologist Bernard-Philippe Groslier may have shed the most light on Angkor's demise. The theory suggests that the Angkorian civilization was "defined, sustained, and ultimately overwhelmed by over-exploitation and the environmental impacts of a complex water-management network." Its vast waterworks proved too great for the city to manage. Also, supplying such a massive empire with water had adverse effects on the environment. Ecological problems included deforestation, topsoil degradation, and erosion due in part to clearing vegetation for cropland. Thus, the city inadvertently brought about its own environmental collapse.

With the use of aerial photography and high-resolution, ground-sensing radar, researchers were able to support Groslier's theory with images that complete existing topographical maps. The radar detected surface structures as well as subtle variances in surface vegetation and soil moisture. This proved that environmental erosion had occurred. The combined images and ground-based investigations further revealed that Angkor was a victim of its own industrial ingenuity, a city ahead of its time and vulnerable to its own power.

▸ **waterworks**
   a water system, including reservoirs, pipes, buildings, and pumps that supply water to a community

▸ **medieval**
   of the Middle Ages time period

▸ **topographical**
   pertaining to the features of the land

1. The author mentions the Khmer Empire in paragraph 1 in order to
   (A) establish the size and importance of the civilization
   (B) explain the downfall of the main city in the empire
   (C) compare the nation's size to a present-day location
   (D) demonstrate why people were not loyal to the city

2. The word speculation in the passage is closest in meaning to
   (A) evidence
   (B) mystery
   (C) question
   (D) growth

3. According to paragraph 2, which of the following is true about the waterworks built within Angkor?
   (A) They transported drinking water to Angkor Wat.
   (B) They were a money-making venture for the city.
   (C) They were built to extend the water supply.
   (D) They irrigated fields along the sides of the river.

4. All of the following are true about the city of Angkor EXCEPT:
   (A) It was built around a water source.
   (B) It had an advanced road system.
   (C) It surpassed other cities of its time.
   (D) It is home to a Buddhist shrine.

5. The word its in the passage refers to
   (A) Angkor's
   (B) baray's
   (C) waterworks'
   (D) home's

6. The word sophisticated in the passage is closest in meaning to
   (A) advanced
   (B) fantastic
   (C) educated
   (D) thorough

7. Which of the sentences below best expresses the essential information in the highlighted sentence? Incorrect choices may change the meaning in important ways or leave out essential information.
   (A) Archaeologists built a replica of what Angkor looked like.
   (B) Archaeologists uncovered the overgrown city and rebuilt its sites.
   (C) Finding the city, workers cleared the forest and studied the architecture.
   (D) The city's architecture was inspired by the forest regions nearby.

8. What can be inferred from paragraph 4 about the people who inhabited Angkor?
   (A) They worshipped ruler Jayavarman VII.
   (B) Hinduism was central to their way of life.
   (C) Religion led to more violence among them.
   (D) They were unified regardless of national religion.

9. Look at the four squares [■] that indicate where the following sentence could be added to the passage.

   These natural catastrophes would have likely resulted in destroyed buildings, ruined crops, and a decreased water supply that would have forced citizens to leave.

   Where would the sentence best fit?

   (A) First square
   (B) Second square
   (C) Third square
   (D) Fourth square

10. The word inadvertently in the passage is closest in meaning to

    (A) purposely
    (B) freely
    (C) sadly
    (D) accidentally

11. According to paragraph 7, which of the following did researchers prove about Groslier's theory with the use of aerial photography and advanced radar?

    (A) The surface soil showed evidence of dirt washing away.
    (B) The waterworks were filled with topsoil.
    (C) Vegetation was thriving where soil was deeper.
    (D) Soil damage was stable throughout the changes.

12. **Directions:** Complete the table below to categorize information about each of the theories discussed in the passage. Match the appropriate statements to the theory with which they are associated. TWO of the answer choices will NOT be used. *This question is worth 4 points.*

Theory	Statements
War Theory	• •
Religion Theory	• •
Groslier's Theory	• • •

Answer Choices

(A) The predominant religion was originally Hindu.
(B) The developments were too vast to manage.
(C) Ongoing attacks weakened the city.
(D) Powerful rulers made Angkor a prosperous city.
(E) The irrigation system sapped the city of its resources.
(F) Thai soldiers invaded and looted the city.
(G) The city's land was eroded and overused.
(H) Architectural projects divided the people.
(I) The change to Buddhism destroyed the people's unity.

03 Astronomy

Magnetars

In 1979, scientists detected a sudden spike in gamma rays that had never before been experienced. Over the next several years, scientists detected that the same unidentified celestial body sent out powerful bursts intermittently. Scientists struggled to determine what was causing these large bursts. They theorized that whatever it was, it had to have a super-strong magnetic field in order to release the amount of energy that it did. By the time another burst was detected in 1998, scientists had come up with an explanation to explain this strange anomaly. The source of these large bursts was termed a magnetar.

A magnetar is defined as a type of neutron star that possesses the strongest magnetic field of anything in space. A refrigerator magnet measures 100 Gauss while the Earth's magnetic field is .5 Gauss. A magnetar measures an amazing 10^{15} Gauss, making it *at least* one hundred trillion times (100,000,000,000,000) as powerful as Earth's magnetic field. Occasionally, these magnetars will experience sudden "bursts" and hurl bright flashes of gamma rays into space. Not much is known about the mechanisms that cause these magnetar "bursts," except that they result from the instability of the star's powerful magnetic field. One theory speculates that the unstable magnetic field causes the star's crust to fold and crack, further disrupting the star's magnetic field and generating massive waves that release large amounts of gamma rays into space.

Although the actual theory was proposed in 1992, magnetars have not yet been categorized as a recognized major type of star. A magnetar is, however, classified as a subtype of neutron star. A neutron star is formed when a massive star dies by collapsing into a supernova or stellar explosion. The mass of a neutron star is greater than the mass of the sun, but is contained in a star with a diameter of only ten to fifteen miles, about the size of Manhattan Island in New York. This extremely dense star is composed mostly of neutrons and has a very strong magnetic field. A magnetar has a magnetic field one thousand times stronger than any other type of neutron star. This gives it an extraordinary amount of power for such a tiny star.

Normal magnetars can generate the amount of energy in one second that it takes the sun a year to produce. ■ **A)** However, the magnetar bursts in 1979 and 1998 were abnormal even for magnetars because they were approximately one thousand times brighter than a normal magnetar. In fact, during the brief period of these outbursts, the magnetars were brighter than supernovas. ■ **B)** The energy that radiates from supernovas in the short period between when they explode and when they fade is equal to the amount of energy the sun will radiate over ten billion years. ■ **C)** Yet the two abnormally strong magnetars of 1979 and 1998 surpassed supernovas in both brightness and energy. ■ **D)** Magnetars are also unique because they produce multiple bursts of light that last only a second, much like a pulsar. A pulsar is a periodic flash of light from a star that is sending a constant beam of energy or light away from itself. Due to the pulsar's rotation, it appears to be blinking on and off as its light sweeps over Earth.

Scientists predict that there are likely millions of magnetars in the galaxy, but only five magnetars have been discovered since the first one was observed in 1979. A recent magnetar was observed in late December 2004. This burst is considered the brightest burst ever. It was only .25 seconds long, but it was powerful enough to overwhelm energy detectors on the many satellites in space so that no energy measurement could be taken. It also interfered with radio communication on Earth. The magnetar was an estimated thirty to fifty thousand light years from Earth. Scientists say that the magnetic force is so strong on a magnetar that it could wipe a credit card clean, or make it ineffective, from a distance of one hundred thousand miles, or about half the distance to the moon.

Although scientists have only been able to detect a few young magnetars, they expect to detect many more in the future. Much about magnetars remains a mystery, and they are a challenge for scientists to study since they appear once every few years and are observable only for a second. Scientists hope to determine more about what causes the instability within a magnetar's magnetic field so that they can better understand these powerful bursts.

▶ **gamma ray**
   a type of radiation with a short wavelength that can pass through solid objects

▶ **celestial**
   in or relating to the sky, heaven, or space

▶ **crust**
   the thick outer surface of a planet

1. The word intermittently in the passage is closest in meaning to

    (A) on a frequent basis
    (B) occurring repeatedly
    (C) not occurring quickly
    (D) not happening regularly

2. The word it in paragraph 1 refers to

    (A) spike in gamma rays
    (B) unidentified celestial object
    (C) energy
    (D) magnetic field

3. The word anomaly in the passage is closest in meaning to

    (A) something out of the ordinary
    (B) an irregular occurrence
    (C) something never seen before
    (D) a natural event

4. Why did the author discuss a refrigerator magnet in paragraph 2?

    (A) To provide a point of reference for a magnetar's strength
    (B) To illustrate that Earth's magnetic field is not as strong as most magnets
    (C) To demonstrate that a magnet has an unstable magnetic field
    (D) To contrast the strength of magnets in space and on Earth

5. According to paragraph 2, magnetar bursts are a product of

    (A) combined magnetic forces
    (B) a weakening of a star's magnetic field
    (C) stars folding into each other
    (D) an unstable magnetic field

6. Which of the following best expresses the essential information in the highlighted sentence? Incorrect answer choices change the meaning in important ways or leave out essential information.

    (A) The disruption in the magnetic field leads to the release of gamma-ray bursts.
    (B) Folds in the star's crust create massive waves that make the magnetic field unstable.
    (C) The star's magnetic field becomes too unstable to be contained within the magnetar.
    (D) The magnetic force causes the star's surface to break into gamma-ray bursts.

7. According to paragraph 3, a magnetar

    (A) has a tiny mass
    (B) is a dying star
    (C) was once a small star
    (D) is larger than Manhattan

8. The author's description of neutron stars mentions all of the following EXCEPT:

    (A) They are formed when a supernova collapses.
    (B) They are the brightest stars that have been discovered.
    (C) They have a huge mass in a small body.
    (D) They have extremely powerful magnetic fields.

9. Look at the four squares [■] that indicate where the following sentence could be added to the passage.

These supernovas have been some of the most luminous events ever observed in the universe.

Where would the sentence best fit?

(A) First square
(B) Second square
(C) Third square
(D) Fourth square

10. Which of the following can be inferred from paragraph 4 about magnetars?

(A) Most magnetar bursts are abnormal.
(B) Pulsars share many similarities with supernovas.
(C) Pulsars and magnetars do not rotate.
(D) Normal magnetar bursts are not as bright as supernovas.

11. Which of the following is NOT true about magnetars in paragraph 5?

(A) The brightest magnetar burst was only .25 seconds long.
(B) The universe is thought to have at least one million magnetars.
(C) The brightest magnetar is thirty to fifty thousand light years away.
(D) Scientists have identified a total of five magnetars since 1978.

12. In paragraph 5, the word it refers to

(A) magnetic force
(B) credit card
(C) magnetar
(D) radio communication

13. Directions: An introductory sentence for a brief summary of the passage is provided below. Complete the summary by selecting the THREE answer choices that express the most important ideas in the passage. Some answer choices do not belong in the summary because they express ideas that are not presented in the passage or are minor ideas in the passage. **This question is worth 2 points.**

This passage discusses a new subtype of neutron star called a magnetar.

-
-
-

Answer Choices

(A) Characterized by their powerful magnetic fields, magnetars are subtypes of neutron stars.
(B) Neutron stars come into being when a massive star dies in a stellar explosion and sends charged matter into space.
(C) Pulsars are similar to magnetars in that their energy beam seems to flash periodically.
(D) The magnetic force on a magnetar is stronger than any other magnetic field in the universe.
(E) Magnetars break brightness records previously set by supernovas and are many times brighter than the sun.
(F) The Earth's magnetic field seems weak in comparison with the magnetic field of a magnetar.

04 Music

Leitmotif

The chords struck in Beethoven's composition for string quartets and the ominous music that fills moviegoers with dread when the villain Darth Vader enters the scene in the *Star Wars* movies are examples of leitmotifs. First coined as a musical term in 1871, it is defined as the leading theme in a piece of music. Taken from the German words *leiten*, which means "to lead," and *motiv*, which means "motive," the word is literally translated as "leading motive." A more modern definition is a dominant recurring theme associated with a person, subject, or idea in a work of art. Leitmotifs are seen across many genres, including music, visual arts, and literature.

A leitmotif is usually a short melody that is repeated throughout the body of a piece of music, though some composers choose to use recurrent chords or percussion rhythms. The use of leitmotifs helps to show congruency within the piece of music and tie the different movements together as a unified whole. The leitmotif usually plays on the emotions of the audience, even if subconsciously, and is a way to convey meaning without words or to take the composition to a different level. Classical music most often comes to mind when leitmotifs are mentioned. They are seen in operas and other dramatic compositions.

■ **A)** A leitmotif cannot be seen in a single song. ■ **B)** For instance, the rhythmic background of hip-hop music is not considered a leitmotif because it does not express emotion or work to change the mood of the song. ■ **C)** A true leitmotif is more than just a style of music; rather, it occurs several times throughout a composition, expressing certain emotions and binding the entire work together. ■ **D)**

The idea of leitmotif can be seen in the music of modern movies, television shows, and even video games. The example of the music played when Darth Vader comes on screen in *Star Wars* is a more classical example of a leitmotif. Likewise, the eerie sound that is played in the *Friday the 13th* horror movie series when the murderer is about to take another victim is a leitmotif as well, though not true music. Both signify the presence of a lead character and evoke intense emotion. Television shows usually use leitmotifs from episode to episode. For example, the television series *Lost* has several leitmotifs that are played at different points in the show. If the actors are climbing or hiking through the thick jungle of the island, the audience hears music that allows it to experience the hard work and time it takes to fight through the dense vegetation. The popular 1990s comedy series *Seinfeld* uses a rhythmic melody for scene changes during each episode. Video game fans can easily recognize the theme music from the *Halo* series played at the beginning of each game.

Leitmotif is not confined only to music, but can be seen in visual works of art. For example, Michelangelo is known for incorporating images of the nude male body in many of his most famous works. His sculpture of David and his painting of the Sistine Chapel both exemplify this image. A more modern artist, Thomas Kinkade, is known as the painter of light. Each of his works includes pastel colors and scenes that seem to reflect and even produce light within the painting. He also paints with themes of simplicity in most of his works. Much of his art features cottage-style homes and simplistic gardens and streams that evoke emotions of comfort and <u>nostalgia</u>.

Literature is another art form in which leitmotifs are used. When employed in literature, a leitmotif is seen as a recurring event, object, or character referred to throughout the book. Author James Joyce's book *A Portrait of the Artist as a Young Man* includes themes of the Virgin Mary and Daedalus from Greek mythology to promote unity as the main character matures. John Grisham, a modern-day writer of fiction, includes themes of ethical dilemma and justice throughout his suspenseful thrillers that deal with the US legal system.

Classical music introduced the idea of leitmotifs to the world, but artists took this concept and applied it to other genres as well. The idea of a recurring theme appealed to artists and audiences alike because it conveyed intense emotion and drew the audience into the drama and beauty of the artistic piece. Leitmotifs have influenced how people participate in art, whether through the emotion of the music or through identifying themes within visual art and literature.

▶ **nostalgia**
a mixed feeling of happiness, sadness, and longing when recalling a person, place, or event from the past

1. The word coined in the passage is best defined as
   (A) named
   (B) enjoyed
   (C) displayed
   (D) invented

2. The word congruency in the passage is closest in meaning to
   (A) symmetry
   (B) regularity
   (C) unity
   (D) similarity

3. Which of the following is NOT correct about the use of a leitmotif in music?
   (A) It is a melody that repeats throughout the work.
   (B) It can be a specific recurring rhythm.
   (C) It ties the various movements together.
   (D) It is used in all forms of music.

4. The word They in paragraph 2 refers to
   (A) Classical music
   (B) Leitmotifs
   (C) Emotions of the audience
   (D) Compositions

5. Look at the four squares [■] that indicate where the following sentence could be added to the passage.

   Similarly, a leitmotif does not flow through all of an artist's songs in the same genre, such as country or rock.

   Where would the sentence best fit?
   (A) First square
   (B) Second square
   (C) Third square
   (D) Fourth square

6. The word composition in the passage is closest in meaning to
   (A) harmony
   (B) book
   (C) make-up
   (D) piece

7. Why does the author mention the *Friday the 13th* horror movies?
   (A) To provide an example of a leitmotif that is not actual music
   (B) To demonstrate the use of a recurring theme within a series
   (C) To illustrate how music can frighten audiences
   (D) To compare the emotions displayed with those in *Star Wars*

8. What can be inferred from paragraph 4 about leitmotifs in movies?
   (A) They affect viewers more than plot development in movies.
   (B) They could be effectively incorporated into romance movies.
   (C) Those used in movies differ from the original definition of leitmotif.
   (D) They ensure an emotional performance on the part of the actor.

9. The word it in paragraph 4 refers to the
   (A) island
   (B) audience
   (C) music
   (D) thick jungle

10. In terms of leitmotifs, the painting on the Sistine Chapel and the sculpture are similar because
    (A) they both feature recurring images
    (B) they are both Michelangelo's work
    (C) they are from the same time period
    (D) their inclusion of nude males is controversial

11. According to paragraph 5, which of the following is true of Thomas Kinkade's work?

(A) He paints scenes from his life in a cottage-style home.

(B) His art causes viewers to think back to their childhood.

(C) His work looks best in pastel light.

(D) He paints cottages where he lived as a child.

12. Which of the following best expresses the essential information in the highlighted sentence? Incorrect answer choices change the meaning in important ways or leave out essential information.

(A) Leitmotif is popular for its ability to articulate feelings that pull the listeners into the dramatic storyline.

(B) The sentiment of the art piece depends on leitmotif to ensure the audience understands what the composer is trying to convey.

(C) Audiences like leitmotif because of the many feelings that are evoked by the story.

(D) Leitmotif is a good idea because audiences and composers can agree on its usefulness.

13. Directions: An introductory sentence for a brief summary of the passage is provided below. Complete the summary by selecting the THREE answer choices that express the most important ideas in the passage. Some answer choices do not belong in the summary because they express ideas that are not presented in the passage or are minor ideas in the passage. ***This question is worth 2 points.***

This passage discusses the extensive use of leitmotifs, or recurring themes, throughout different types of art.

-
-
-

Answer Choices

(A) Thomas Kinkade uses leitmotifs in his paintings through light and through simple, cozy scenes as subjects.

(B) Though leitmotifs are seen mostly in music, they are often used in literature and visual art.

(C) A leitmotif is usually a link between separate movements of music, chapters in a book, scenes of movies or TV shows, or an artist's works.

(D) Theme music in movies and TV is an example of the use of leitmotifs in modern expressions of art.

(E) A leitmotif cannot be seen in a single song because it is more than a foundational rhythm or music in a chorus.

(F) Leitmotifs are a way to communicate intense emotion and bring about a different scene without explicitly explaining what the artist has in mind.

05 Biology

Neurons and Human Memory

Writing a paper, recognizing a smell, remembering a phone number, and singing a song are all examples of different functions that require some measure of human memory. The processes of the brain have puzzled and intrigued scientists for years. Many have sought to understand how the memory works. After years of study, research shows that memory is recorded and processed by neurons found in the brain.

Neurons, or nerve cells, are the basic units of the nervous system. These cells comprise the core components of the brain and act as the processing and transmission centers for the body. They are the way the rest of the body communicates with the brain and are highly specialized in nature. Some neurons in the brain are capable of signaling and connecting with thousands of other cells. Others receive many signals, but only send out one or two. A synapse is essentially a gap between neurons that serves as the link between them. These neurons transmit information across the synapse in the form of an electrical impulse. It is within the action of these neurons that memories are created.

Memory is the ability to store, retain, and retrieve information. For the brain to record memories, it requires a simultaneous and coordinated activation of neuron receptors at the synapses. For example, a child knows not to touch hot objects from a previous experience of being burned. When he first touched a hot stovetop, the pain signal from the skin on his hand along with the view from his retina reached the brain at the same time, forming a memory. He refers to that memory each time he sees a hot object, remembering the consequences of touching something hot. Thus, the signals sent to the neurons in the brain formed a specific and useful memory.

One researcher has studied the basic functions of memory, finding that individual memories are "burned onto" receptors that are constantly in motion around nerve synapses. ■ **A)** The synapses allow signals to travel through the brain, and often the receptors containing memories are lost or escape from the synapses. ■ **B)** When this occurs, a specific set of molecules catches the loose receptors and takes them to a recycling plant of sorts, where they are reprocessed and then returned intact to the synapse. ■ **C)** When the receptors are not recycled, there is a gradual loss of synaptic function and, subsequently, a reduced cognitive ability. These findings may prove useful in understanding memory loss as well as neurological disorders such as Alzheimer's and learning disorders like autism. ■ **D)**

A different group of scientists has performed a study on the specific connection between memory and neurons. The study showed that when a person learns something and then recalls what was learned, the same neurons used in the original experience are triggered. It actually reintroduces the same emotions felt when the memory was formed. Additionally, memories are most likely stored in neuron subgroups. Those neurons are activated in response to various sensory experiences that prompt a memory. This discovery shows precisely which circuits are active during formation of a specific memory. Whereas researchers previously knew that neurons existed, they now understand more comprehensively how they work.

This study was done on a set of mice that contained a specific gene that had been altered for study. In essence, the scientists genetically tagged, or marked, individual neurons within each mouse's brain and noted when the neurons were activated within a given time frame. They reasoned that fear was a natural and necessary emotion in survival and thus was a valid emotion that mice experience. The technology allowed scientists to record and measure neuron activity along with certain memories. The mice showed that the same neurons activated during fear conditioning are reactivated during memory retrieval.

Now that researchers have found a link between neurons and memory formation, the technique can be applied in other settings. The procedure could help physicians discover how medications work in the brain. Until now, physicians have had trouble evaluating the effects of antidepressants on patients because each patient can react differently to a medication. Antidepressants that work for one individual may not work for another. Often, physicians can measure the effects of antidepressants on a patient only after months of observation. This new genetic tagging technology would allow physicians to evaluate treatment by comparing how a patient's brain works at two different times during treatment, noting how and where the drug affects specific neurons. This would allow physicians to evaluate treatment options more quickly and accurately.

▶ **retina**
the part at the back of the eye that sends light signals to the brain

▶ **cognitive**
related to memory, reasoning and judgment

▶ **sensory**
relating to the senses or transmitting sensation

1. The word intrigued in the passage is closest in meaning to
   (A) busied
   (B) fascinated
   (C) informed
   (D) taught

2. The word They in paragraph 2 refers to
   (A) Components of the brain
   (B) Basic units
   (C) Neurons
   (D) Processing and transmission centers

3. According to paragraph 2, what makes nerve cells within the brain unique?
   (A) They form the body's nervous system.
   (B) They receive signals from the rest of the body.
   (C) They are dependent on synapses to give them information.
   (D) Their only function is to store memories.

4. The word simultaneous in the passage is closest in meaning to
   (A) singular
   (B) painful
   (C) clear
   (D) instant

5. Why does the author mention the child who touched a hot object?
   (A) To argue that the action was done purposely to form a useful memory
   (B) To illustrate a memory that can prevent repeated action
   (C) To compare touching hot objects with the formation of negative memories
   (D) To note a symbolic way that the brain records memories

6. According to paragraph 3, all of the following are true of memory formation EXCEPT:
   (A) It results in the storage and retention of events.

(B) Consequences of an action are not recorded as memory.
(C) Simultaneous and coordinated activity is required.
(D) The process involves information moving across synapses.

7. Look at the four squares [■] that indicate where the following sentence could be added to the passage.

   This is an ongoing process occurring over minutes or hours, so the brain continually receives recycled receptors.

   Where would the sentence best fit?
   (A) First square
   (B) Second square
   (C) Third square
   (D) Fourth square

8. Which of the following can be inferred about neurological illnesses?
   (A) The recycling of receptors leads to Alzheimer's and other diseases.
   (B) The cause of these illnesses is not treatable because it involves neurons.
   (C) "Burning" neurons results in a mass of memories that move as one group.
   (D) Loss of receptors is a likely cause of these brain disorders.

9. According to paragraph 5, how does emotion from an experience factor into memory?
   (A) Feelings are reintroduced when recalling the specific memory.
   (B) The brain records the emotion that becomes the memory.
   (C) Memory-related feelings are only recalled in certain circuits.
   (D) Neurons activate the appropriate emotion depending on the type of memory.

10. The word prompt in the passage is closest in meaning to

(A) happen quickly
(B) arrive on time
(C) come together
(D) bring around

11. The word they in paragraph 5 refers to

(A) memories
(B) researchers
(C) neurons
(D) circuits

12. The author discusses fear conditioning in paragraph 6 in order to

(A) illustrate one of the multiple techniques used to test the mice
(B) demonstrate a logical emotion to which mice respond
(C) explain the only feeling recorded by active neurons
(D) question the researchers' techniques and findings

13. Which of the sentences below best expresses the essential information in the highlighted sentence? Incorrect choices may change the meaning in important ways or leave out essential information.

(A) Physicians can see how medication affects the brain and which drug is most effective by using this technology.
(B) The new technology allows doctors to diagnose certain illnesses and then treat them with a variety of drugs.
(C) By monitoring the patient's brain, doctors can experiment with different drugs and note their effect on each patient.
(D) Patients subject to tagging technology show notable brain activity and are more resistant to medication.

14. Directions: An introductory sentence for a brief summary of the passage is provided below. Complete the summary by selecting the THREE answer choices that express the most important ideas in the passage. Some answer choices do not belong in the summary because they express ideas that are not presented in the passage or are minor ideas in the passage. ***This question is worth 2 points.***

Studies show that the link between memory formation and neurons is the recording of an experience and related emotions through the transmission of information from the body to the brain.

-
-
-

Answer Choices

(A) Electrical impulses are the way in which information travels from neuron to neuron.
(B) New tagging technology offers information about how and when a neuron is activated.
(C) The body's nervous system involves neurons, the brain, and nerves throughout the body.
(D) Researchers found that when a memory is recalled, the associated feeling is experienced.
(E) Memories are stored in neuron subgroups once they are recorded.
(F) Neurons transfer information, but they also record events to be stored in the brain.

Developing Skills for the

TOEFL® iBT

Second Edition

Intermediate

READING

Paul Edmunds · Nancie McKinnon · Jeff Zeter

Answer Key

Answer Key

Note: Graphic Organizer answers are suggestions only and may not match students' answers exactly.

Preview Test

1. (D)	2. (B)	3. (B)
4. (A)	5. (A)	6. (B)
7. (B)	8. (C)	9. (A)
10. (C)	11. (D)	12. (C)
13. (A)	14. (A, C, F)	

Chapter 1 Fact Questions

01 Linguistics

The Effect of the Gold Rush on the English Language	
Theory	Example
Many English expressions originated during California Gold Rush	"Pan out" came to mean "to be successful"
	"Strike it rich" came to mean "to become wealthy"

1. (C)   2. (B)   3. (D)

Summary: The passage discusses English phrases that can be <u>traced</u> back to the gold rush in California. The phrase "pan out" came from the pans that miners used. Gold would <u>settle</u> to the bottom of their pans, and the sediment would be removed. The expression "<u>strike</u> it rich" originated from miners striking the rocks to find gold and becoming <u>wealthy</u> quickly if they found it.

02 Theater

The Greek Chorus and the Audience	
Definition	Role
Person or group of people that added to a play in various ways	Helped audience understand play by providing important plot information
	Interacted with audience, either by showing emotion or by communicating with audience members

1. (D)   2. (C)   3. (B)

Summary: The role of the chorus in Greek theater was to provide a <u>commentary</u> on a play to the audience in order to <u>clarify</u> the plot. The chorus explained the stories and <u>facilitated</u> the audience's understanding of events. By singing or speaking in <u>unison</u>, the chorus was also responsible for influencing the way audiences reacted to a play. It did this by showing <u>embellished</u> reactions and discussing the play's events and characters with the audience.

03 Ecology

Changes in Coral Reefs	
Cause	Effect
1. Increased ocean temperatures	Bleaching of coral occurs when it loses algae
2. Tropical storms	Sediment fills water and blocks sunlight, causing algae to die

1. (B)   2. (A)   3. (D)

Summary: Global warming is responsible for <u>altering</u> the ocean's temperatures, which affects coral reefs. Coral reefs are <u>vulnerable</u> to temperature changes, and they become damaged if exposed to higher temperatures for <u>prolonged</u> periods. One <u>indication</u> of coral damage due to warm ocean temperatures is bleaching. An increase in tropical storms is another way coral reefs are being damaged because of global warming. Sediment from overflowing rivers <u>clouds</u> the ocean, which decreases the amount of sunlight reaching the corals.

04 Literature

The Romance vs. The Novel		
The Romance	Both	The Novel
• Moral stories of heroic adventures	• Popular in 15th century	• Stories of everyday life
• Used language considered lofty		• Used language considered low
• Idealized portrayal of characters		• Realistic portrayal of characters

1. (A)   2. (D)   3. (B)

Summary: The passage discusses the appearance of the novel as it <u>flourished</u> along with the romance in the 15th century. The invention of the printing press increased the <u>distribution</u> of written texts to people. The novel often <u>parodied</u> the impossible characters and formal style of the romance, instead presenting more realistic <u>temperaments</u> and motives of people. Also, the main <u>focal</u> point of the novel was character, as opposed to plot in the romance.

05 Anthropology

Symbolic Behavior	
Theory	Support
Superstitions can have positive psychological effects	1. Rituals can give sense of control over uncertain situations
	2. Taboos can relieve anxiety in many situations

1. (B)   2. (A)   3. (C)

Summary: The passage discusses symbolic behavior as a means for people to <u>cope</u> with uncertainty in their lives. Two common types of <u>symbolic</u> behavior are rituals and taboos. Rituals are behaviors done repeatedly in order to bring about a certain <u>outcome</u>. Although a ritual cannot <u>solely</u> bring about a desired result, an individual can get a feeling of control through performing the ritual. Taboos are forbidden behaviors that can make some people believe that something terrible will <u>transpire</u>. By avoiding a certain taboo, a person may feel that he or she can also avoid misfortune.

06 Sociology

Globalization	
Cause	Effect
1. Dutch East India Company began worldwide export activity	Beginning of globalization
2. Traded with nations previously closed to trade, increasing cultural mixing	

1. (A)   2. (A)   3. (D)

Summary: The passage discusses the Dutch East India Company as an important <u>impetus</u> in the trend of globalization beginning in the 17th century. It provided an <u>avenue</u> for cultural exchanges through the trade of goods by sea. Through their <u>maritime</u> trade abilities, the Dutch grew in power and eliminated competition by <u>expelling</u> the Portuguese and the British from the East Indies. Through the trade activities of the Dutch East India Company, highly prized and exotic items such as spice and textiles were able to <u>circulate</u> around the world.

01 Psychology

Conversation: Men vs. Women		
Men	Both	Women
• More likely to make conversation fun and make jokes • Do not generally chat with male friends often	• Conversation has similar goals	• More likely to discuss problems and emotions • Often call friends just to talk

1. (C)   2. (B)   3. (D)

Summary: According to the passage, men and women <u>engage</u> in very different same-sex conversations. For men, talk is generally not personal, is more likely to include <u>innocent</u> teasing and joking, and is not very common. Men often consider personal feelings a sign of <u>vulnerability</u>. By contrast, women often <u>broach</u> personal topics such as feelings and problems with one another. Female conversation is thought to be very important to maintain and <u>nurture</u> female relationships.

02 Agriculture

Water Shortage	
Problem	Solution
Agricultural waste of water	1. Use underground watering to reduce evaporation and runoff
	2. Grow native plant species that thrive in an environment

1. (D)   2. (C)   3. (D)

Summary: The passage discusses ways in which farmers are trying to <u>counter</u> shortages of clean, fresh water. When crops are watered above the surface of the ground, much of the water <u>evaporates</u> instead of reaching the plants. By installing new underground irrigation systems, a more <u>uniform</u> application of water can reach the root systems of the plants. Another <u>novel</u> idea for farmers to use water more efficiently is to grow more native species of crops. Native crops can grow without excessive watering, thus slowing the <u>depletion</u> of precious water resources.

03 Marketing

Product Demonstration		
Definition	Advantage	Example
Giving customers an opportunity to experience the product in person	1. Can make a product more real to a customer, which can increase sales	Car dealers often give test drives to customers
	2. Can demonstrate unique benefit or function of a product	Sales of a company's cookware went up after demonstrating its benefits

1. (D) 2. (D) 3. (B)

Summary: According to the passage, while product advertising is <u>advantageous</u> in selling goods and services, a hands-on demonstration is often more effective with <u>prospective</u> customers. Product demonstration makes an item more <u>tangible</u> to buyers, in that they can actually touch and use it before they buy it. This shows <u>consumers</u> what a product's function is, which can lead to higher sales of the product. For example, a manufacturer of non-stick cookware made many more sales after demonstrating its product at an <u>exposition</u>.

04 Political Science

Dependency Theory		
Theory	Support	Example
Developing nations cannot progress while remaining dependent on other nations	Developing nations spend more on imports than on exports	Grenada exports bananas, nutmeg, and cocoa but must import many other products

1. (C) 2. (A) 3. (A)

Summary: The passage discusses dependency theory, which explains why some developing nations cannot <u>integrate</u> into the world economy. These countries will not succeed economically until they <u>restructure</u> their import and export programs. Because the <u>revenue</u> gained from exports is much lower than the <u>expenditures</u> needed to import basic goods, these nations cannot generate a healthy economy. Dependency theorists suggest that the only <u>viable</u> solution for these countries is to increase manufacturing in order to decrease dependence upon developed nations for their welfare.

05 Anthropology

Cultural Interpretations	
Ethnocentrism	Cultural Relativism
Judges cultures based on one culture's standards	Judges cultures based only on that culture's standards
Von Däniken did not believe ancient Egyptians built pyramids	Egyptians must have built pyramids

1. (C) 2. (D) 3. (D)

Summary: The passage discusses two ways in which cultures can be understood. The first is ethnocentrism, which is the interpretation of a culture based on the <u>standards</u> of one's own culture. Ethnocentrism is thought to be a <u>universal</u> occurrence. Another way to interpret cultures is cultural relativism, which judges cultures according to their own standards. However, this <u>position</u> can be difficult to adopt without <u>extensive</u> effort and study of other cultures. Anthropologists help <u>alleviate</u> this problem.

06 History

The History of the Globe Theatre		
Step 1: Built in 1599 but burned down in 1613	Step 2: Rebuilt in 1614 but closed down and demolished	Step 3: Replica built in 1997 to match original

1. (A) 2. (C) 3. (D)

Summary: According to the passage, London's famous Globe Theatre has a complex and <u>illustrious/turbulent</u> history <u>spanning</u> about 400 years. Constructed as an open-air amphitheater, its center was a large pit in which <u>attendees</u> would stand and watch the performances. After it was destroyed twice, it existed only in the minds of its <u>admirers</u> for 350 years. Finally in 1997, the Globe Theatre was again rebuilt. It is an open-air <u>venue</u>, just like the original.

01 Literature

Unreliable Narrators	
Definition	Role
Narrator who does not describe events truthfully	1. Make readers question story and narrator
	2. Add realism to characters

1. (D) 2. (A) 3. (D)

Summary: According to the passage, an unreliable narrator is a literary device that is used to challenge the reader's trust. Unreliable narrators are also used by authors to add a sense of realism to a character. The example used is "The Cask of Amontillado" by Edgar Allen Poe. The unreliable narrator in this case is Montresor, whose view is tainted with prejudice and a desire for revenge. Readers must contemplate whether or not to believe the unreliable narrator, thereby gaining a more comprehensive understanding of the character.

02 Business

Successful Entrepreneurship	
Requirement	Example
1. Innovation	Amazon.com made buying books more convenient
2. Risk-taking	Debbi Fields took risks to finance cookie chain

1. (D) 2. (B) 3. (D)

Summary: According to the passage, entrepreneurialism is the launching of a business venture in order to make money. Two factors that can bring about success in new business are innovation and risk-taking. Innovation is crucial in fulfilling a unique public demand. Risk-taking is another necessary component of a new business because many entrepreneurs are competing in a new or difficult territory. For example, the owner of a successful cookie chain had to convince a bank to finance her business concept in order to become successful.

03 Biology

The Botanical Career of Carl Linnaeus		
Step 1: Developed love for plants and began to name and classify them	Step 2: Went on expeditions to find new plant species and developed *Systema Naturae*	Step 3: Became professor and lcontinued to gather plant species from around the world

1. (D) 2. (B) 3. (D)

Summary: According to the passage, Carl Linnaeus was a botanist who dedicated his life to creating a classification system of plants. The process began with a love of plants as a child. Linnaeus set out on many expeditions to find new plants. As a professor, he gained worldwide renown and collected many plant specimens from around the world. His *Systema Naturae* grew considerably into a multivolume work that was preserved by other scientists after his death.

04 Psychology

Fuzzy Trace Theory		
Definition	Category	Example
False memories are created due to brain making traces of events	1. Gist trace: trace of basic idea of an entire event	Soccer player may remember how a game went but forget specific details
	2. Verbatim trace: trace of specific details of an event	Patient may remember specific details from an event but forget event itself

1. (A) 2. (C) 3. (D)

Summary: According to the passage, the phenomenon of generating false memories can be explained by the fuzzy trace theory. This theory states that after an experience, the brain makes traces of information. A gist trace is a remembrance of the event in a general sense. Because the brain remembers a general sense of the entirety of an event rather than specific details, false memories may be created to fill in the gaps. A verbatim trace is a recollection of events based on specific details or moments, rather than the experience as a whole.

05 Astronomy

Lunar Craters	
Type	Explanation
1. Impact craters	Form from meteorites and asteroids crashing into surface of moon
2. Volcanic craters	Magma under surface breaks through and causes surface to collapse

1. (C)   2. (A)   3. (D)

Summary: The moon has accumulated a number of craters that form its jagged <u>terrain</u>. The <u>vast</u> majority of lunar craters are caused by the impact of meteorites and asteroids. Because the moon has no atmosphere, there is no protective <u>barrier</u> to burn up meteorites before they hit the moon's surface. Therefore, when meteorites explode upon impact, surface material is <u>ejected</u> with great force. Another way lunar craters are formed is when <u>molten</u> rock rises through the moon's surface, breaking it. A cavity forms beneath the surface, which eventually collapses to form a crater.

06 Zoology

Wolves and Dogs	
Theory	Support
Modern dogs retain many characteristics of wolves	1. Both form hierarchical relationships
	2. Both are territorial and can be aggressive

1. (A)   2. (B)   3. (D)

Summary: According to the passage, while dogs and wolves bear little physical <u>resemblance</u> to each other, they demonstrate common traits. For example, their social structures consist of hierarchies within packs or families. They are also both highly <u>territorial</u> and become aggressive to assert dominance and ownership. Wolves and many dogs have an <u>inherent</u> <u>belligerence</u> toward strangers. They react to a threat by <u>baring</u> their teeth and displaying other aggressive behavior.

Chapter 4   Rhetorical Purpose Questions

01 Literature

Identifying Theme	
Step 1: Examine title for clues	Step 2: Look for repeated words or images

1. (B)   2. (C)   3. (B)

Summary: The focus of the passage is on literary themes and how to <u>interpret/discern</u> themes in poetry. A theme is the general idea that is expressed in a poem. The author describes two ways of <u>discerning/interpreting</u> themes in poetry. First, the reader can analyze a title, which often <u>indicates</u> what the poem may be about. For example, Lewis Carroll's "A Boat beneath a Sunny Sky" suggests that the poem is about something joyful and <u>tranquil</u>. Next, the reader should look for repeated words or images, as they often help the reader <u>conclude</u> the theme of the poem.

02 Meteorology

How Aurora Borealis Is Formed		
Step		
1. Sun discharges plasma	2. Plasma reaches Earth's atmosphere	3. Plasma particles collide with atmospheric gases
Description		
Plasma is made up of particles	Plasma travels through space; eventually comes into contact with atmosphere	Gas atoms build up energy; release it as light

1. (D)   2. (A)   3. (D)

Summary: According to the passage, many of the <u>spectacular</u> weather phenomena seen from Earth are caused by powerful storms in space. For example, Aurora Borealis is an extra-planetary storm that results in the appearance of <u>impressive</u> lights in the northern sky. Aurora Borealis is caused when particles are <u>discharged</u> from the sun. Then, the particles <u>collide</u> with gases in the Earth's atmosphere. In the process, an electric charge is transferred to the gases. The collision causes energy to build up. When the energy is released, the gases emit lights with a continuously changing <u>spectrum</u> of colors.

03 Environmental Science

Electric Cars	
Theory	Support
Electric cars are better for the environment and economy	1. Study showed electric cars reduce carbon dioxide emissions by 100 percent
	2. Reduce influence of petroleum prices on world economy
	3. Less expensive to operate

1. (C)   2. (A)   3. (B)

Summary: The invention of the automobile has had a profound effect on modern transportation. The passage describes the merits of the electric car and its benefits to the environment and the economy. Gasoline engines produce gases and fumes that contribute to global warming. Electric cars, meanwhile, can reduce emissions by one hundred percent. Electric cars are also better because they reduce reliance on petroleum. Decreased dependence reduces the impact of fluctuating petroleum prices on the economy.

04 Biology

Altruism and Evolution		
Theory	Explanation	Example
Kin Selection	Animal sacrifices chances of reproducing or surviving to help evolutionary success of species	While some bees do not reproduce, this actually helps species to survive

1. (A)   2. (B)   3. (D)

Summary: The passage discusses altruism in biology. Altruism, or selfless behavior, is considered an evolutionary mechanism that seems to defy the theory of natural selection. Some scientists believe that by exercising kin selection, some animals promote the genetic fitness of their species by sacrificing themselves. For example, worker bees forgo their ability to reproduce so that they can protect the hive and their queen.

05 Oceanography

How Rogue Waves Are Formed	
Theory	Support
1. Wave interactions with ocean currents	1. Agulhas Current runs past southern tip of Africa, a region with a high incidence of rogue waves
2. Wave reinforcement	2. When two or more waves join, their respective heights add together

1. (C)   2. (B)   3. (A)

Summary: According to many personal accounts and mathematical calculations, rogue waves can reach incredible heights. Stories of rogue waves have circulated for centuries, but scientists still are not sure what causes them. A high incidence of rogue waves off the southern tip of Africa seems to be caused by contact between normal wave patterns and ocean currents. In other areas, rogue waves may be caused by two or more waves joining together to form one massive wave. However, the exact circumstances in which rogue waves appear are still unknown, and in fact, they may sometimes occur randomly.

06 Anthropology

Native American Pottery		
Type	Materials	Technique
1. Southwestern	Dry clay	Use of extremely hot temperatures
2. Northeastern	Many different materials	Mix materials with clay, use of coil technique, rub with stones

1. (A)   2. (C)   3. (D)

Summary: The passage discusses artifacts recovered in the southwestern and the northeastern parts of the United States. A popular and revered art form, the pottery of southwestern Native Americans has an extensive history. In the beginning, they created more functional pottery out of clay, subjecting it to extremely hot temperatures. Northeastern pottery featured many different materials due to disparate geography. Native Americans in the northeast also finished pots with stones to add a polished look.

| Vocabulary Review 1 |

1. (B)	2. (D)	3. (C)
4. (D)	5. (A)	6. (C)
7. (D)	8. (B)	

9. (C)	10. (A)	11. (B)
12. (D)	13. (B)	14. (A)
15. (C)		

16. phenomenon	17. spectacular	18. discharge
19. gap	20. indication	

21. (C)	22. (A)	23. (E)
24. (B)	25. (D)	

| Mini Test 1 |

01 Environmental Science

1. (D)	2. (D)	3. (B)
4. (B)	5. (D)	6. (C)
7. (B)	8. (C)	

02 Marketing

1. (C)	2. (D)	3. (A)
4. (C)	5. (A)	6. (A)
7. (D)	8. (D)	

Chapter 5 Vocabulary Questions

01 Linguistics

Vocabulary	
Type	Point
1. Passive Vocabulary	1. Larger than active vocabulary
	2. Expands as a person ages
2. Active Vocabulary	1. Smaller than passive vocabulary
	2. Limited by words needed to communicate

1. (C)	2. (B)	3. (A)

Summary: The passage describes two different types of vocabulary that <u>linguists</u> recognize. Passive vocabulary is the set of words that a person knows but <u>avoids</u> using in speech or writing. A person's <u>passive</u> vocabulary expands throughout his or her <u>lifetime</u>. Active vocabulary, on the other hand, is the set of words that a person can actually <u>produce</u> when speaking or writing.

02 Biology

Angiosperms			
250 Million Years Ago	130 Million Years Ago	100 Million Years Ago	80 Million Years Ago
Gigantopterids contained chemicals used by angiosperms	Earliest angiosperm fossil	Bees helped angiosperms spread	Angiosperms became most common type of plant

1. (A)	2. (B)	3. (B)

Summary: The passage discusses angiosperms, flowering plants that continued to <u>thrive</u> long after dinosaurs became extinct. The earliest angiosperm <u>fossil</u> is thought to be 130 million years old. It is also <u>estimated</u> that angiosperms began to evolve about 250 million years ago from the gigantopterids. Gigantopterids may be the earliest <u>ancestor</u> of angiosperms. Bees helped the plants <u>diffuse</u> across the world by spreading the plants' pollen. Angiosperms are now the most common type of plant on Earth.

03 Economics

Inflation	
An increase in prices of all goods and services	
Demand-pull inflation	Cost-push inflation
People "bid up" price of goods, causing companies to charge more	Rising production costs drive up general prices

1. (C)	2. (D)	3. (B)

Summary: The passage discusses two economic theories explaining inflation. The first is demand-pull inflation. This is when supplies are unable to meet consumer demand. By their willingness to pay more for the product, consumers <u>effectively</u> bid up the price. Factors causing demand-pull inflation include an increase in currency or <u>exports</u>. The second type of inflation is cost-push inflation. This occurs when the <u>production</u> price of something increases. Companies must charge consumers more in order to keep the businesses <u>profitable</u>. Cost-push inflation can also be caused by an increase in the price of <u>raw materials</u>.

04 Photography

Contrast		
Step	Description	Example
1. Lighting	The way light hits subject affects contrast	To increase contrast, photographer can use colored lens filters
2. Exposure	Amount of light that hits film affects color	To ensure proper exposure, photographer can bracket shot

1. (C)   2. (A)   3. (B)

Summary: The passage describes ways that photographers can achieve effective contrast in photographs. Proper contrast in a photograph will <u>direct</u> the viewer's attention to its most interesting aspects. One way is to <u>regulate</u> the amount of time the film is exposed to light. By using lens <u>filters</u>, photographers can accentuate certain colors and reduce others. The other way that photographers control contrast is by exposing the film correctly. Exposure can be <u>manipulated</u> by changing the aperture or the shutter speed. A technique called bracketing can allow a photographer to choose an exposure that will <u>render</u> the best contrast in a photograph.

05 Health

Fatigue		
A condition of extreme sleepiness or exhaustion		
Physical Fatigue	Mental Fatigue	Pathological Fatigue
Person cannot perform at usual level	Sleepiness or lack of concentration	Caused by disease

1. (B)   2. (A)   3. (B)

Summary: The passage discusses three types of fatigue, the feeling of extreme <u>weariness</u> or exhaustion. Physical fatigue can be described as feeling <u>drained</u>, and is caused by physical exertion. This type of fatigue is a <u>temporary</u> loss of muscle function, and is usually pronounced after some type of <u>exertion</u>. The second type is mental fatigue. It is characterized by feelings of <u>drowsiness</u> and difficulty concentrating. The third type is pathological fatigue, which may be caused by a disease such as chronic fatigue syndrome.

06 Anthropology

Origin of Austronesian Languages		
Theory	Support	Explanation
Austronesian languages originated in ancient Taiwan	1. Nine of ten Austronesian languages formed from Formosan languages	Formosan languages spoken by Taiwanese aborigines
	2. Austronesian peoples migrated from Taiwan	Migration patterns prove Austronesian-speaking peoples are genetically and linguistically related to Taiwanese aborigines

1. (A)   2. (C)   3. (C)

Summary: The passage proposes that the often-<u>ignored</u> aborigines of Taiwan are the descendants of the original speakers of Austronesian languages. Anthropologists have uncovered evidence that <u>confirms</u> the origins of this language family. The most convincing data <u>stems</u> from the fact that languages usually originate in areas with the most linguistic <u>diversity</u>. Studies reveal that Formosan languages form nine out of the ten branches of Austronesian language. Scientists also can genetically link peoples from countries that speak Austronesian languages to the ancient inhabitants of Taiwan by studying their <u>migration</u> patterns.

Chapter 6   Reference Questions

01 History

The Formation of the United Nations			
1919	1943	1944	1945
League of Nations sets the stage for future organizations	During talks, leaders agree to create international organization	Five nations meet to discuss goals of organization	United Nations convenes for first time

1. (C)   2. (B)   3. (A)

Summary: The passage discusses the history of the United Nations. Another international organization called the League of Nations <u>preceded</u> its formation, but it had been ineffective in <u>enforcing</u> its resolutions. World leaders wanted to avoid another <u>devastating</u> world war, so they made an agreement to create a new peacekeeping organization. After a series of <u>wartime</u> conferences with representatives from around the world, the United Nations officially <u>convened</u> for the first time on October 24th, 1945.

02 Sociology

Urbanization in Mexico City	
Problem	Solution
1. Water shortages	Seek new sources for water and increase public awareness about water conservation
2. Heavy traffic	Improve public transportation to reduce traffic

1. (C) 2. (C) 3. (A)

Summary: The passage discusses the problems associated with urbanization. A large population shift from <u>rural</u> communities to large cities can cause great difficulties, especially in areas where population growth <u>surpasses</u> a city's ability to meet the needs of its citizens. For example, in the <u>metropolis</u> of Mexico City, issues such as water <u>shortages</u> and heavy traffic are a challenge for city officials. Mexican administrators are now exploring options that will provide people with a safe and <u>reliable</u> water supply and efficient public transportation.

03 Astronomy

Binary Star Systems	
Classification	Explanation
1. Visual	Can be seen with a telescope
2. Spectroscopic	Can only be seen with a spectrometer
3. Eclipsing	Continuously eclipse each other as they orbit around center of mass

1. (B) 2. (C) 3. (C)

Summary: Pairs of stars that <u>orbit</u> around the same center of mass in space are called binary star systems. The point that the mass of a system is <u>concentrated</u> on is the binary star system's center of mass. Visual binary stars can be seen through a telescope with high <u>resolving</u> power. Spectroscopic binary stars can only be seen with a spectrometer, which measures <u>unperceivable</u> differences in the light the stars emit. Eclipsing binary stars travel along an orbit in which they eclipse each other. Studying eclipsing binary stars allow scientists to determine the <u>composition</u> of space.

04 Biology

Plant Movements		
Type	Characteristic	
1. Tropisms	1. Directional reaction to stimulus	
	2. Irreversible	
2. Nastic Movements	1. Response to environmental stimulus	
	2. Reversible	

1. (C) 2. (D) 3. (A)

Summary: While plants may appear to be <u>stationary</u> objects, they do in fact move a great deal. For example, ivy plants can <u>interweave</u> with a pole, and sunflowers <u>crane</u> their faces toward the sun. One type of plant movement is tropism. Tropisms occur when a plant reacts to a directional <u>stimulus</u>. For instance, phototropism is when a plant moves in response to a light stimulus. Another type of plant movement is nastic movement. It occurs when a plant reacts to environmental changes. Thigmonasty occurs when the plant moves in response to touch. This movement is a <u>mechanism</u> that allows plants such as the Venus flytrap to feed.

05 Health Sciences

Effects of Sugar	
Theory	Support
1. Sugar is psychologically addictive	Surveys reveal that people seek sugary food to improve mood and become anxious without it
2. Sugar is physically addictive	Studies show that rats become addicted and experience withdrawal symptoms if sugar is taken away

1. (B) 2. (D) 3. (A)

Summary: The passage discusses the theory that sugar can be addictive. When a person <u>craves</u> sugary foods and experiences a negative reaction in its absence, he or she may have a sugar addiction. Although sugar cane has been <u>cultivated</u> for thousands of years, too much sugar can cause tooth decay and <u>suppress</u> the immune system. According to surveys, people <u>indulge</u> in sugary foods when they are feeling angry or sad. This suggests that sugar is psychologically addictive. Evidence that it may also be physically addictive was revealed after a study on rats. The rats that were dependent on sugar experienced <u>tremors</u> and other withdrawal symptoms when the sugar was taken away.

06 Psychology

How Pfungst Discovered the Clever Hans Effect			
Step			
1. Pfungst removed Hans from audience to ask questions	2. Pfungst had people aside from Hans's trainer ask questions	3. Pfungst asked questions without Hans seeing him	4. Pfungst had people ask Hans questions to which they did not know answers
Result			
Hans answered correctly	Hans answered correctly	Hans performed poorly	Hans performed poorly

1. (A)　　　2. (C)　　　3. (B)

Summary: The passage discusses a psychological phenomenon called the Clever Hans Effect. It was discovered by German psychologist Oskar Pfungst when he documented the case of a horse that could allegedly perform arithmetic and keep track of the date. In order to showcase his amazing skills, Clever Hans and his owner traveled the continent. Pfungst subjected the horse to a series of tests and discovered that the horse was actually just adept at interpreting human body language. By being more receptive to cues from the trainer's involuntary body language, Clever Hans was able to produce the correct answers.

Chapter 7	Sentence Simplification Questions

01 Geography

The Rain Shadow Effect			
Step			
1. Water on surface evaporates	2. Moist air rises and cools	3. Cold air causes water vapor to condense and produce precipitation	4. Mountains block rain from reaching leeward side, creating rain shadow

1. (C)　　　2. (A)　　　3. (D)

Summary: The passage discusses the rain shadow effect, which occurs when the hydrologic cycle is interrupted. When the water in the air evaporates, the moist air rises. When it reaches the high elevation of a mountain range, the cooler temperatures cause it to condense. Usually, water droplets fall back down to the ground as precipitation after they evaporate. However, if a mountain physically obstructs the rain clouds, the rain will fall before it can reach the other side. Therefore, the water never returns to that area.

02 Business

The Online Auction Business Model	
Advantage	Disadvantage
1. No time or geographic constraints	1. Decreased consumer confidence because of criminal activity
2. High level of consumer loyalty	2. Need for increased Internet security

1. (D)　　　2. (C)　　　3. (B)

Summary: The passage is about the online auction business model, which allows people to bid on and purchase items via the Internet. The business model has both advantages and disadvantages. The model does not have the time or geographic constraints of other businesses, and it provides high customer loyalty. However, the anonymity of patrons allows for such criminal activities as the sale of stolen or counterfeit items.

03 Biology

Species Related to Amphibian Evolution		
Species		
1. Crossopterygian fish	2. *Panderichthys*	3. *Ichthyostega*
Description		
Primitive feet; similar skull and teeth to amphibians	Flat bodies, straight tails, and more developed feet	First true amphibian; had legs and lungs

1. (D)　　　2. (A)　　　3. (D)

Summary: The passage is about the evolution of amphibians, which are cold-blooded animals that hatch in water and are born with gills. Few fossils of early amphibians have been found, but scientists have managed to determine some transitional species among them. From the earliest ancestor, the crossopterygian fish, scientists observed the development of feet-like apparatus. Later, the *Panderichthys* fish was found to have amphibian-like features, unlike its earlier counterparts. Finally, the fossils of the *Ichthyostega* are believed to be the first proper amphibian.

04 History

What Caused the Fall of Rome?	
Theory	Support
Roman society became too complex to sustain itself	In an attempt to solve food shortages, Romans conquered other nations, but as empire grew bigger and more complex, it did not have resources to sustain itself

1. (C)   2. (A)   3. (D)

Summary: The passage is about Joseph Tainter's theory regarding the fall of the Roman Empire. This great civilization has been studied by many scholars. According to Tainter, Roman society was ruined because it became too complex. Complex societies need resources to finance the costs of solutions to their problems. In an attempt to address their food shortage, the Romans decided to conquer neighboring lands and take their resources. Eventually, the Romans only created more problems for themselves and extended their resources until they could no longer maintain the society.

05 Psychology

Intelligence		
Type		
1. Analytical	2. Creative	3. Contextual
Details		
Related to skills taught in school	Ability to apply knowledge to new situations	Ability to make changes to succeed in any context

1. (D)   2. (C)   3. (A)

Summary: The passage is about Robert Sterberg's Triarchic Theory of Human Intelligence. His approach studies three components of intelligence: analytical, creative, and contextual. Analytical intelligence is measured by proficiency in academic tasks, and is often determined through the use of standardized tests. Creative intelligence is how well a person can apply known skills to new situations. Often, creatively intelligent people are quite intuitive. Contextual intelligence is the ability to behave appropriately in any given context.

06 Anthropology

Cultural Diffusion	
Type	Explanation
1. Direct contact diffusion	Culture close to another adopts an aspect of other culture
2. Intermediate contact diffusion	"Middlemen" help spread part of a culture to other areas
3. Stimulus diffusion	One culture's technology prompts similar technology in another culture

1. (C)   2. (B)   3. (D)

Summary: The passage discusses cultural diffusion, when aspects of a culture are incorporated into another. There are three different modes of cultural diffusion. Direct contact diffusion occurs when one culture takes on aspects of a culture that it has contact with. Intermediate contact diffusion is when the spread of a culture happens through a "middleman." Stimulus diffusion is when the knowledge of a certain trait spurs the invention of a similar trait in another culture, though it may not be an exact replica.

Chapter 8   Text Insertion Questions

01 Biology

Fungi	
Characteristic	Role
1. Decompose organic material to gain nutrients	Allow nutrients to be returned to soil through decomposition
2. Reproduce through spores put into the air	Reproduce very quickly, which led to their use in medicine

1. (D)   2. (B)   3. (C)

Summary: According to the passage, although fungi can be a nuisance, they are vital to ecosystems. Despite their destructive capabilities, fungi help to decompose organic matter so that nutrients will be returned to the environment. In addition, fungi exhibit reproductive behavior through the use of spores. Once the spores find a habitable area, they reproduce very quickly. This reproductive ability has led to their use in the development of antibiotics in modern medicine.

02 Business

Product Stewardship		
Definition	Aspect	Role
Reducing a product's environmental impact throughout life cycle	1. Manufacturer participation	Use safe packaging and encourage recycling
	2. Retailer participation	Aid manufacturers in getting message to consumers
	3. Government participation	Encourage recycling and create statewide programs

1. (D)   2. (C)   3. (A)

Summary: The passage discusses the concept of product stewardship. It encourages environmental protection plans that are implemented throughout a product's entire life cycle. Manufacturers have begun using new packaging that is recyclable and non-toxic. Retailers are also acting as mediators between manufacturers and consumers. They are also executing/instating recycling programs. Lastly, state governments are fostering recycling through many programs, such as the container deposit program.

03 Astronomy

The Runaway Greenhouse Effect	
Cause	Effect
1. Greenhouse gases trap solar radiation, preventing heat loss	Temperature on Venus becomes very high
2. Heat causes oceans to evaporate, water vapor escapes atmosphere	No water remains on Venus

1. (C)   2. (D)   3. (A)

Summary: The passage discusses the runaway greenhouse effect on Venus. Greenhouse gases serve to heat both Earth and Venus. However, their atmospheres are much different despite their relative proximity to each other. Venus's high concentration of carbon dioxide acts as a barrier. This exacerbates the heating effect by preventing the sun's infrared radiation from escaping Venus's atmosphere. The heat caused by the gases allowed water to evaporate and escape the atmosphere, which is why oceans never formed on Venus.

04 History

Olmsted and Public Space		
Topic	Point	Explanation
Olmsted changed the way public spaces were viewed	1. Thought public spaces should provide escape from city life	Made Central Park resemble New York as little as possible while remaining cohesive part of city
	2. Thought public spaces should be for everyone	Ensured Central Park was in a location that everyone could get to easily

1. (C)   2. (B)   3. (C)

Summary: The passage discusses the changes in public spaces effected by landscape architect Frederick Law Olmsted. He realized that cities lacked a cohesive balance of places in which to work, play, and live. Olmsted planned Central Park in New York around the idea that people needed a sanctuary in order to escape the bustle of city life. While previous public spaces had catered to certain groups of people, Olmsted wanted Central Park to be accessible to all members of the public.

05 Psychology

Selective Attention Theories		
Theory	Explanation	Example
1. Filter Theories	Brain filters unnecessary information	In a crowded room, you will not hear every conversation, but will recognize your name
2. Attentional resource theories	Attention is fixed amount to divide among tasks	In a crowded room, one must divide attention among events

1. (B)   2. (C)   3. (A)

Summary: The passage discusses selective attention theories, which try to determine why people focus their attention in different ways. Filter theories say that the brain filters out unwanted information. For example, a person disregards conversations in a room if they have no relevance to his or her thoughts. One's brain can filter unfamiliar information and redirect attention to familiar names or voices. Attentional resource theories describe attention as a fixed amount to divide according to how much attention one wants to pay to something. A person can devote a certain amount of attention to certain stimuli.

06 Literature

Allegory		
Definition	Role	Example
Use of extended metaphor in a story	1. To describe difficult concepts	Plato's allegory of prisoners in a cave to describe philosophical knowledge
	2. To tell familiar story in new way	George Orwell's allegory of animals on a farm to describe a political situation

1. (B)　　2. (B)　　3. (C)

Summary: The passage discusses the use of allegory in literature. Allegory is used as an extended metaphor for two reasons. The first is to explain difficult concepts. For example, Plato uses the <u>bondage</u> of prisoners to explain philosophical knowledge. The second purpose of allegory is to tell a familiar story in a new way. For instance, in George Orwell's *Animal Farm*, farm animals <u>stage</u> a revolution to <u>evict</u> humans from their farm. They soon discover that they are not <u>fit</u> to run the farm themselves. The story's events <u>figuratively</u> represent the political situation of Orwell's time.

| Vocabulary Review 2 |

1. (B)　　2. (D)　　3. (A)
4. (D)　　5. (D)　　6. (A)
7. (C)　　8. (B)

9. (A)　　10. (A)　　11. (B)
12. (D)　　13. (C)　　14. (B)
15. (A)

16. Fossils　17. preserved　18. devote
19. identifying　20. instrumental

21. (B)　　22. (E)　　23. (C)
24. (A)　　25. (D)

| Mini Test 2 |

01 Zoology

1. (B)　　2. (C)　　3. (D)
4. (B)　　5. (C)　　6. (A)
7. (B)　　8. (D)

02 Linguistics

1. (B)　　2. (C)　　3. (C)
4. (C)　　5. (A)　　6. (B)
7. (A)　　8. (A)

01 Botany

Plant Stems		
Definition	Part	Function
Plant structure that supports buds and leaves and carries nutrients to plant	1. Phloem	Carries carbohydrates from leaves to roots
	2. Xylem	Water and nutrients pulled from roots to leaves

1. (A, C, D)

Summary: Stems are the support structure for a plant's buds and leaves. <u>Concentric</u> rings within the stem transport nutrients downward from the <u>source</u> to the plant's roots through the pressure-flow mechanism. Water evaporates from the leaves, which <u>attracts</u> more water molecules upward from the roots. This process creates <u>tension</u> in the interior of the stem for continuous water movement. More water enters through the roots from the soil, <u>sustaining</u> the life of the plant.

02 Archaeology

Experimental Archaeology		
Definition	Role	Example
Subfield of archaeology that attempts to replicate ancient processes	Reveals new information about ancient cultures	Paint-making using primitive methods and materials

1. (A, B, E)

Summary: Experimental archaeology attempts to <u>replicate</u> certain skills of past cultures. By doing this, we can determine what made ancient artifacts so <u>durable</u>. Archaeologists use only the <u>primitive</u> materials and methods available at the time the items were made. One experiment recreated the process of paint-making using ores, minerals, and <u>sedimentary</u> deposits. Then, animal fat was <u>extracted</u> using tools available at the time. Finally, yucca roots were added to recreate the substance likely made by ancient paint makers.

03 History

Entrepreneurship During the California Gold Rush		
Cause	Effect	Example
California Gold Rush	Increase in entrepreneurial opportunities	Levi Strauss capitalized on needs of gold miners

1. (C, D, F)

Summary: The 1849 gold rush in California inadvertently created opportunities for entrepreneurs to make their fortunes in ways other than mining. A rapidly growing population increased the demand for basic necessities such as food and clothing. While some merchants inflated their prices to take advantage of the miners' plight, many were honest and hardworking. Levi Strauss was a merchant who sold various types of apparel, including a type of work trousers that used metal rivets. This provided a type of pants that fulfilled miners' needs in a new way and led to his success.

04 Astronomy

Why the Sky Is Blue	
Theory	Support
Molecules in the atmosphere scatter color in sunlight	1. Rayleigh discovered sunlight is scattered by water molecules in atmosphere
	2. Rayleigh found that light scattered is mostly in blue part of spectrum, giving sky blue color

1. (B, E, F)

Summary: The sky appears to be blue because of the scattering of light waves against water molecules in the atmosphere. The colors of the light spectrum we can see range from red, which has the longest wavelength, to violet, which has the shortest. When light rays are broken or refracted by water in the atmosphere, colors appear separated because of their wavelengths. The scattering of light molecules in the sky is predominantly at the blue end of the light spectrum because of its shorter wavelength, most easily seen by the human eye. Farther from the sun, the greater saturation of color makes the sky appear a deeper blue.

05 Art History

Stieglitz Photography		
Definition	Role	Example
Photography as art rather than production of standard photographs	Promoted artistic side of photography	*Equivalents*—images of shadow and light to capture moment of experience

1. (B, C, F)

Summary: Alfred Stieglitz was a photographer who made his work an expression of artistic interpretation of the world around him. Dada art had a profound impact on the way he viewed photography, so he became interested in the promotion of photography as art. Stieglitz edited and published a photography periodical and focused much of his work on urban surroundings. His *Equivalents* series was intended to completely capture a moment in time, thereby affording the viewer an equivalent experience of the feeling of that moment.

06 Sociology

The Role of the Media in Socialization	
Advantage	Disadvantage
1. Educate children about academic and social skills	1. Show violence, which can teach the wrong lessons
2. Provide common topics to discuss	2. Depict stereotypes that are learned and believed by public

1. (C, D, E)

Summary: The passage discusses the media's role in socialization, which has only intensified as television's role has grown in society. Television is undeniably an important part of modern culture. The media have educational and interactional advantages and disadvantages. Many people believe that the media help educate children and give people common topics to discuss in social settings. However, others believe that the media promote violence and implant often unrealistic stereotypes.

Chapter 10 Table/Chart Questions

01 Geology

Seismic Waves	
Classification	Attribute
1. P Waves (Primary Waves)	1. The fastest waves
	2. Can travel through any medium
	3. Vibrate in the direction they travel
2. S Waves (Secondary Waves)	1. Slower than P waves
	2. Travel through only solid mediums
	3. Vibrate at right angles

1.

Seismic Wave	Statements
P waves	• Produce vibrations that move in the direction of the waves • Move through underground water • Are the fastest moving waves
S waves	• Can only move through solids • Produce vibrations that move up and down or side to side

Summary: According to the passage, earthquakes generate shock waves known as seismic waves. Two kinds of seismic waves travel through the Earth's interior. Primary waves, or P waves, travel outward from where an earthquake originates. They can move through solids, liquids, or gases under the surface of the Earth, alternately compressing and expanding them. S waves are secondary waves that can only move through solids. They vibrate at right angles to their direction. S waves travel more slowly than P waves and can only travel through solid mediums. Scientists can compare S waves and P waves to pinpoint the location of earthquakes, even thousands of miles away.

02 Anthropology

Hunter-Gatherers vs. Pastoralists		
Hunter-Gatherers	Both	Pastoralists
• Egalitarian society • Basic unit is band • Lots of social mobility among bands	• Based on small groups	• Hierarchical • Extended family headed by father • Part or all of group moves with herd

1.

Society	Statements
Hunter-Gatherer	• A married woman has a choice of several different groups with whom she can live. • Members of the group are treated as equals.
Pastoralist	• Herds often split into groups that move separately. • About 12,000 years ago, humans thought to develop this method. • Sons usually live in a group with their fathers, even after they marry.

Summary: The way in which a pre-industrial society finds or produces its food affects its social structure. Hunter-gatherer societies, in which members forage for food, are egalitarian. Members are usually related through marriage or kinship. Everyone gets an equal share of the meat, and they can easily move from one band to another. Pastoralist societies are hierarchical. Usually an older male member heads up the group, which consists of his sons and their families. Pastoralists also rely on domesticated animals for food and other products.

03 Philosophy

The Philosophies of Plato and Aristotle		
Problem	Theory	Explanation
What is the best form of government?	1. Philosopher-king	Only philosopher can understand ideal of good life
	2. Rule of law	Even ruler must be subject to laws

1.

Philosopher	Statements
Plato	• Only a philosopher can understand the ideal of the good life. • The world of Forms is the true reality. • Rule of law is necessary for good government in the absence of a philosopher-king. • A world exists that is beyond the human senses.
Aristotle	• Man perceives reality through his senses. • A government based on the rule of law is the best method. • Even rulers must follow the laws of the state.

Summary: According to the passage, Plato believed reality existed in a world of Forms that could only be understood by philosophers. Because human senses cannot give a perfect <u>rendering</u> of the world, it is only through the mind that humans can truly know reality. For Plato, the ideal form of government was a philosopher-king, who could <u>ensure</u> that the concept <u>derived</u> from the world of Forms was promoted. Without a philosopher-king, Plato believed that the rule of law was the <u>subsequent</u> form of good government. Aristotle, however, believed that what people perceived through their senses was reality. His theory that even rulers must follow the rule of law formed the <u>underpinning</u> of constitutional governments today.

04 Art History

Baroque vs. Rococo		
Baroque	Both	Rococo
• Very large buildings • Bright colors • Impressive views	• Integration of painting, sculpture, and architecture	• Less imposing, smaller scale • Pastel tones • Unified interiors

1.

Architectural Style	Statements
Baroque	• Palaces were especially massive and imposing. • Different, dramatic views were used in the design of the interior. • Paintings using bright colors decorated church interiors.
Rococo	• Swirls and curves were used in interior design. • Sculptures tended to be smaller and less dramatic.

Summary: There are four key elements of Baroque architecture. Buildings were massive. Architecture, painting, and sculpture worked together. The interiors used bright colors and different materials, and there were dramatic views off the main visual <u>axis</u>. Baroque architecture was too <u>robust</u> for the tastes of the time. However, Rococo architecture was a <u>refinement</u> of these elements. Its decoration was more delicate and <u>subtle</u>. It also featured the <u>integration</u> of painting and sculpture with its architecture.

05 Sociology

The Changing Ideas of Race		
Meaning		
1. People who shared same identity or way of life were called a race	2. Race was characterized by physical attributes	3. Race is cultural idea that has no biological basis

1.

Period	Concept of Race
Original Usage	• Said that a race of people shared a lifestyle
16th and 17th Centuries	• Divided people into races according to physical traits • Stated that parents pass racial characteristics to their children
20th Century	• Proved that races are not determined by biology • Described race as a cultural creation

Summary: According to the passage, it was <u>conventional</u> wisdom that race simply <u>denoted</u> a group of people who shared an identity, such as being from the same country. Race meant something much different from its current <u>association</u>. Later, people thought race was a biological fact. It was believed that certain physical and behavioral traits could be used to <u>distinguish</u> each race. Finally, scientists showed there was no scientific basis for the idea of race, and it was actually a cultural <u>construct</u>.

06 Economics

Keynes vs. Friedman		
Keynes	Both	Friedman
• Money supply does not affect economy • Key to strong economy is demand • Spending will create demand and strengthen economy	• Based on quantity theory of money	• Money supply affects economy • Contraction of money supply caused Great Depression • More money available for spending increases health of economy

1.

Theory	Statements
Keynesian	• Governments can change tax policies to change consumer spending. • The employment rate will fall without sufficient demand. • The health of an economy depends on three kinds of spending.
Monetarist	• Governments need to control the supply of money in order to affect the economy. • The economy will be negatively affected by a contracted supply of money.

Summary: Two economists developed new theories on how governments can influence the economy. Keynesian economists believe that three <u>variables</u> affect economic activity: consumer spending, government spending, and investment. Keynes's theories became so widely accepted that economists rejected <u>monetary</u> policy to manage economic activity. On the other hand, Friedman's monetarists believe that money supplies have a <u>causal</u> effect on the economy. They attribute the <u>fiscal</u> disaster of the Great Depression to a <u>contraction</u> in the money supply, causing the market to decline.

| Vocabulary Review 3 |

1. (B) 2. (D) 3. (A)
4. (B) 5. (C) 6. (A)
7. (D) 8. (C)

9. (A) 10. (B) 11. (B)
12. (D) 13. (C) 14. (D)
15. (A)

16. denotes 17. construct 18. underpinning
19. stereotypes 20. ranking

21. (B) 22. (C) 23. (A)
24. (E) 25. (D)

| Mini Test 3 |

01 Health

1. (B, C, E)

02 Business

1. (B, E, F)

03 Biology

1.

Infectious Agents	Characteristics
Virions	• Can be prevented before infection • Include a piece of genetic material that is replicated
Prions	• Cause irreversible damage to tissues • Are composed of matter found in the body • Form an abnormal and irregular structure

04 History

1.

Theory	Statements
Chicxulub Theory	• A piece of a large asteroid may have broken away in space and hit Earth. • An object from outer space left a crater on the Yucatan Peninsula. • Dinosaurs became extinct because of a meteor's impact on Earth.
Keller's Theory	• Global warming caused by volcanic activity contributed to extinction. • Volcanic eruptions released toxic gases and caused acid rain. • Dinosaur species weakened after years of stressful living conditions. • The Earth was bombarded by multiple meteors that diminished dinosaur numbers.

| Practice Test |

01 Psychology

1. (B) 2. (C) 3. (B)
4. (B) 5. (C) 6. (A)
7. (A) 8. (B) 9. (A)
10. (C) 11. (D) 12. (B)
13. (B, D, E)

02 History

1. (A) 2. (C) 3. (C)
4. (B) 5. (C) 6. (A)
7. (B) 8. (B) 9. (C)
10. (D) 11. (A)

12.

Theory	Statements
War Theory	• Ongoing attacks weakened the city. • Thai soldiers invaded and looted the city.
Religion Theory	• The predominant religion was originally Hindu. • The change to Buddhism destroyed the people's unity.
Groslier's Theory	• The developments were too vast to manage. • The irrigation system sapped the city of its resources. • The city's land was eroded and overused.

03 Astronomy

1. (D)	2. (B)	3. (A)
4. (A)	5. (D)	6. (A)
7. (B)	8. (B)	9. (B)
10. (D)	11. (D)	12. (B)
13. (A, D, E)		

04 Music

1. (D)	2. (C)	3. (D)
4. (B)	5. (C)	6. (D)
7. (A)	8. (B)	9. (B)
10. (A)	11. (B)	12. (A)
13. (B, C, F)		

05 Biology

1. (B)	2. (C)	3. (B)
4. (D)	5. (B)	6. (B)
7. (C)	8. (D)	9. (A)
10. (D)	11. (B)	12. (B)
13. (A)	14. (A, D, F)